D0560278

REFLECTIONS
ON
CAPTIVITY

REFLECTIONS
ON
CAPTIVITY

A TAPESTRY OF STORIES
BY A VIETNAM WAR POW

PORTER ALEXANDER HALYBURTON

NAVAL INSTITUTE PRESS
ANNAPOLIS, MARYLAND

Naval Institute Press
291 Wood Road
Annapolis, MD 21402

Library of Congress Cataloging-in-Publication Data
Names: Halyburton, Porter, author.
Title: Reflections on captivity : a tapestry of stories by a Vietnam War POW / Porter Alexander Halyburton.
Description: Annapolis, Maryland : Naval Institute Press, [2022] | Includes bibliographical references.
Identifiers: LCCN 2022014243 (print) | LCCN 2022014244 (ebook) | ISBN 9781682478257 (hardback) | ISBN 9781682478448 (ebook)
Subjects: LCSH: Vietnam War, 1961-1975—Prisoners and prisons, North Vietnamese. | Vietnam War, 1961-1975—Prisoners and prisons, American. | Prisoners of war—Vietnam—Biography. | Prisoners of war—United States—Biography. | Hỏa Lò Prison (Hanoi, Vietnam) | Vietnam War, 1961-1975—Personal narratives. | BISAC: BIOGRAPHY & AUTOBIOGRAPHY / Military | HISTORY / Wars & Conflicts / Vietnam War Classification: LCC DS559.4 .H35 2022   (print) | LCC DS559.4   (ebook) | DDC 959.70437092 [B—dc23/eng/20220726 LC record available at https://lccn.loc.gov/2022014243
LC ebook record available at https://lccn.loc.gov/2022014244

♾ Print editions meet the requirements of ANSI/NISO z39.48-1992 (Permanence of Paper).
Printed in the United States of America.

30 29 28 27 26 25 24 23 22   9 8 7 6 5 4 3 2 1
First printing

All images from author's personal collection unless otherwise indicated.

—∞∞∞—

To Marty, my love and guiding star.
Stan Olmstead
Bob Purcell
Mike Christian

CONTENTS

Introduction

FLYING IN COMBAT OVER NORTH VIETNAM IN 1965, I certainly thought there was a chance that I might be killed. Yet, despite the incredible ground fire that we encountered on most bombing runs, the more missions I flew without incident the more remote that danger seemed. To be sure, the threat clearly was evident on my first night mission over North Vietnam: I saw just how much ordnance was being thrown at us. In daytime you saw only the gray puffs of flak from the anti-aircraft artillery, but at night I was awed by the bright orange flashes and the stream of tracers from the smaller guns. How was it possible to fly through all that unscathed? For every tracer round, there were ten or more rounds you did not see. Despite this barrage, I survived seventy-five missions without incident.

Most of the missions I flew seemed a waste of time and money. They had little real effect on the war's outcome, and they certainly weren't worth risking our lives. We searched for trucks carrying arms and supplies destined for Viet Cong units operating in South Vietnam. We bombed small bridges when it seemed worthwhile. But we never saw a single truck; the North Vietnamese quickly rebuilt the bridges; and the other targets that we considered seemed insignificant or inconsequential. Sometimes we did not find any targets at all, and since we couldn't bring our ordnance back onto our carrier lest it explode on board the ship, we had to dump it onto Tiger Island, a small strip of land off the North Vietnamese coast. Since the islet was the assigned dumping ground for all Navy bombers and fighter-bombers in the war zone, it probably accumulated more bombs per square meter than any other spot in North Vietnam.

Finally, on October 17, 1965, our unit—Air Wing 7 on the aircraft carrier USS *Independence* (CVA 62)—was given a significant mission that military leaders said potentially could affect the course of the war. We were ordered to cut off a major supply line between China and Vietnam—by destroying a railway and road bridge in the industrial city of Thai Nguyen, about forty miles north of Hanoi. This was an Alpha Strike and the largest attack against North Vietnam of the war—so far. It would involve strike groups from two carriers, along with Air Force fighter-bombers based in Thailand. Significantly, it was one of those critical targets that could only be attacked with specific permission from president Lyndon B. Johnson and his Secretary of Defense, Robert S. McNamara. (Until then, every strategic target that might have made a difference in the war was off-limits to the generals and admirals, mostly for political reasons.)

This was an important development, because if the United States was ever going to win a military victory over North Vietnam—which was essential if we and

Map shows divided North and South Vietnam and neighboring Laos and Cambodia, all of which played a part in the U.S.-Vietnam War of 1961–75. The Gulf of Tonkin was the scene of the naval skirmish that prompted the United States to intensify its military effort. *U.S. Naval Institute Press*

the South Vietnamese army were ever going to quell the Viet Cong insurgency in South Vietnam—it could not be done under the restrictive rules of engagement that had been placed on the U.S. forces that were charged with conducting the air war. The United States also faced the difficulty of winning a *political* victory in South Vietnam, which was needed to achieve the broader American goal of creating a free, democratic, and prosperous South Vietnam able to defend itself against the communist North and—by extension— to ward off China, the Soviet Union, and the spread of communism.[1]

It was small wonder, then, that Adm. U. S. Grant Sharp, commander in chief of the U.S. forces in the Pacific, appeared at our pre-takeoff briefing before the mission got under way to stress the importance of this joint strike.

This was to be my seventy-sixth combat mission. My squadron, VF-84, known as the "Jolly Rogers," had assigned four F-4B fighter-bombers to flak-suppression duty, arming them with rockets to take out the antiaircraft guns protecting the bridge while the A-4 and A-6 attack aircraft tried to destroy the span with bombs. I was flying with Lt. Cdr. Stan Olmstead, who I considered to be the best pilot in the squadron, and we had flown many missions together.[2]

The strike force of more than thirty aircraft from the *Independence* flew north up the Gulf of Tonkin on that bright Sunday morning. Our F-4B was at the tail end of the group when it entered North Vietnam, about forty miles north of the port city of Haiphong.

Porter (*left*) with pilot Lt. Cdr. Stan Olmstead in front of a Navy F-4B Phantom on the USS *Independence* in 1965.

We were flying at low level to avoid the surface-to-air missiles that defended Haiphong and Hanoi; the Russian-made SAM II missiles could not function in altitudes below three thousand feet. We were deep inside the country on the way to the target when we were struck by antiaircraft fire. Simultaneously, the F-4 being piloted by Tubby Johnson was hit in one of its engines, and he began broadcasting on the radio, "Fire warning light, we are hit, turning back." Fortunately,

VF-84 F-4B Phantom #205, shot down on October 17, 1965. The tail bears the skull-and-crossbones insignia of Navy fighter squadrons VF-84 on the USS *Independence* (CVA 62). *U.S. Navy*

Tubby and his radar intercept officer, Zipper Ward, made it back to the ship on one engine.

Since Tubby's plane and mine were hit at about the same time, there was confusion about what happened. Stan most likely was killed by a direct hit in the front cockpit, and I had no control over the aircraft and could not use the radio, since the oxygen mask containing the microphone had been blown off. With only a few seconds to decide what to do before the plane crashed into the karst ridge directly ahead, I asked myself, "Do I eject now or ride it in with Stan?" I was struck hard by the realization that my life either was over or was about to be changed forever. A thousand thoughts of my family raced through my mind in those few seconds—images of my mother and grandparents; my wife, Marty; and our daughter, Dabney, only six months old. I decided that if there was even a chance of rescue or survival, I had to take it. I reached for the ejection handle and pulled.

The Martin-Baker ejection seat uses an artillery shell that blasts the seat up from the cockpit at a force of twenty gravity forces (known as Gs), instantly increasing a person's relative body weight by twenty times. I have no memory of the moment when I weighed the equivalent of 3,600 pounds, but I had experienced nine Gs before, and it had felt as though my flesh was about to be stripped from my bones.

Seconds later I was floating down into hostile and unknown territory, with bullets popping through the canopy of my parachute. I had gone from the comfort and safety of my aircraft—with its electronic tether back to the ship—into enemy territory, full of uncertainty.

I landed after just a very few swings in the parachute and quickly got rid of the 'chute and other gear that would hamper my escape and evasion. I tried my handheld radio, but got no response. The bullets had come from one direction, so I turned toward the opposite one, hoping to make it over a hill and away from the gunfire. But I quickly ran out of steam and searched for shelter where I could hide and catch my breath. I ran toward the largest group of bushes that I could see, but a very large snake decided he wanted to go there too, so I graciously let him have it and ran to the next-largest group of bushes. Unfortunately, the clump did not provide much concealment. As I heard men approaching, I tried my radio one last time, but again there was no response. I knew that the enemy used captured radios to lure rescue helicopters into traps, so I destroyed mine so it could not be employed that way. The finality of that act quashed my last hope for rescue.

I soon was captured by nearby villagers, who removed my flight vest, G-suit, and boots—everyone was curious about me and all my gear—and escorted me in my sock feet a mile or so to their small hamlet.

In retrospect, I was treated very well. I am sure they had never seen an American before, because there had been little bombing in this area. Placed in the corner of a small shed with three-foot-high mud walls and a thatched roof, I was permitted to keep and smoke my own cigarettes. When I signaled that I was thirsty, I was given water, some rice, and some kind of boiled greens. I ate it all so as not to offend them, and I made up my mind right then that I would eat everything I was given if it would help me to survive.

A short time later soldiers arrived in a Jeep-like vehicle to take me away. The forty-mile trip to Hanoi, motoring over horrible, rutted roads, took two days. Along the way, we stopped at a larger village, where I was put on display like some sort of trophy. The only brick building in the village must have been used for town meetings and as a school. In it I was seated on a wooden bench, and across the table from me was an official of some kind, with a guard standing by the door. There were other Vietnamese in the room as well. The official did not speak English, but he carried a phrase book that he used to copy questions onto a piece of paper. The paper was pushed in front of me along with a pencil, and I was told to write. I pushed the paper back and shook my head "no." This went back and forth several more times, and each time that I refused the interrogator became angrier and angrier. So did the other Vietnamese crowded in the room—especially the guard with an AK-47 assault rifle. He finally became so upset that he rushed over and held the barrel of the gun against my temple and began jamming it into my head. *This is it—he is going to kill me*, I thought, but at that point I had already accepted that fate, since I figured that captivity in this place was going to be worse than death. At one point I noticed that the people standing opposite the guard and me were still standing there, and for a moment I thought that he might be bluffing. Then he chambered a round in the gun, and the people quickly scrambled out of the way—so I said a prayer, closed my eyes, and waited for the shot that would end my life. When it didn't come, I opened my eyes and realized that he had been calmed down and taken outside. When they realized that I was not going to provide any information, I was loaded back in the jeep and we continued our journey, stopping for the night at a small army base. I don't think I slept at all that night; the hard wooden planks that served as a bed were unforgiving, and the thoughts of what lay ahead spun through my mind.

The next day I arrived at Hoa Lo Prison in Hanoi to begin my nearly seven-and-a-half-year imprisonment in North Vietnam.

During those 2,675 days, I was confined in eight different prisons and was moved thirty times. I lived in many different situations—solitary confinement, with one cellmate, with two cellmates, with eight cellmates, and, finally, with groups of up to fifty. Each of these living situations differed radically from the others.

Reflecting on my captivity years later, after I'd been repatriated, I could see how I was able to adapt and react to these situations, changes, and time periods. The adaptations were physical, mental, and spiritual.

In the many speeches and lectures I have given over the years, I've found it useful to talk about my experiences—and the things I learned from them—in terms of three time periods and three phases of adaptation.

The first time period began with my capture in October 1965 and ended with the Hanoi March and my separation from a fellow POW, Maj. Fred V. Cherry, USAF, in July 1966. The second period started when the first one ended—with my move to the Briarpatch prison compound in July 1966—and it did not end until the last days of 1969 and early in 1970. The last period was from early 1970 until my release on February 12, 1973.

The first phase of my adaptation occurred during times when I was concentrating as much as possible on the past—to escape the reality of the present. The second involved striving to live as much as possible in the future—to get away from the present. I spent the third (and last) phase mostly in the present, after I realized I could still lead a meaningful life that did not depend upon my freedom.

When I began writing these stories about my time in prison, I wanted to concentrate on the positive aspects rather than the negative ones. I tried to include tales of great courage and leadership; accounts of creativity, innovation, education, and adaptation; stories about exceptional individuals; humorous incidents; and finally, a look at the things I learned that helped me survive and that still guide my life today.

I have included some of the poetry that I wrote during this time as well as some of the lyrics to the songs that I composed. I kept all of these in my mind, since we did not have writing materials until the very end. This first poem was written early in 1966, when most of us were still optimistic that the war would be over soon. That optimism began to fade that summer, and I knew by then that I had a lot more to do than just wait.

WINTER CRYPT

How can I describe the way that I feel?
As if the stream I was crossing
Had suddenly frozen
And locked my ankles in an icy grip,
Immobilizing that once-fluid force
And I with it. . . .
And we have nothing to do
But wait until the thaw.

Part One

---∞∞∞---

Rolling with the Punches

"You've gotta get there early to get the good deals."
—SAILORS' TONGUE-IN-CHEEK HUMOR

No Such Thing as a Rotten Banana

FROM MY FIRST DAY IN NORTH VIETNAM IN THAT REMOTE village, I ate everything I was given. I did not save food for later. I did not throw any food away. If it was food and I could get it down, I ate it. The exception was "fish crunchies." This supposedly was dried fish, but it was mostly large bones that were too hard to chew up without damage to my mouth or throat, and it had a strong taste of ammonia. The smaller dried fish did not have that taste, and I could chew up the bones except for the eyeballs, which turned to hard little marbles when they dried. There were also rats, snakes, monkeys, ragweed, and all sorts of strange things that I had never heard of, much less eaten.

At first, we were given very stale bread and watery soup, but later the prison cooks replaced the bread with rice. You had to be very careful eating the rice because it often contained small, rice-like rocks, rat turds, and other debris.

If we got any protein at all, it usually was from pig fat. Once, when I was moved from one cellblock to another, I could see a little bit under my blindfold,

13

and as we walked through some weeds I saw what I thought was an old tire, but it got up and walked away. It turned out to be a black pot-bellied Vietnamese pig with a large head, huge belly, and no hams—an animal I had never seen or heard of before. So, this is where the pork came from, I thought, and the Vietnamese were "eating high on the hog" while we were eating low. When we did get the low part, it came in the form of a plug about the size of my thumb. It had a tiny bit of meat on one end and skin with bristles on the other. In between there was an inch of fat. I watched as others removed the skin and threw it away or just plucked out the bristles. I ate it all, of course. After several years, I did a rough calculation of how many footballs and paint brushes could have been made from all the skin and bristles I had eaten. It was a lot.

One of the good things that the Vietnamese learned from the French during the colonial period was how to make bread. One time we got it fresh from the oven, and it was about the best-tasting thing I had put in my mouth in a long time. Most of the time, however, it was stale and moldy, to the point where the outside was hard as a brick and the inside was mushy and a little green. We had a special name for this—"rose bread"—the same that we used for the rotten potatoes we sometimes got; both had a faint rose smell. We sometimes had beans with that rotten rose smell as well.

Then there was the fruit that we occasionally got. Sometimes it was oranges or longan fruit, but mostly it was bananas, and there were many kinds of them. The Vietnamese said there were seven varieties, from the small, fat ones with white, apple-tasting flesh and hard, black seeds—we called them "hand grenades"—to the plantain-sized ones.

The bananas were always welcome, but often they were overly ripe—blackened skins, full of strong custard that many guys either could not or would not eat. I always ate them and just told myself that they had the most flavor, which they did.

Culinary monotony was always a factor, but during the summer of 1967 it became extreme due to the severe drought and the resulting scarcity of food. The only food that was available was poor-quality rice mixed with field corn, yellow squash (pumpkin), and a large green squash. That is all we ate for nearly sixty days.

Anytime we went to interrogation we carried a "bitch-list" in our heads so we could potentially lodge our complaints about the food and other things with the interrogator. Doing so could even divert the subject from what the interrogator wanted to discuss to what we wanted to discuss. Sometimes this worked, but often it did not.

After we complained so much about the lack of salt, the prison staff finally responded by putting a huge amount in the soup one day, making it so salty that we could barely eat it, although I did.

Worse Place, Better Place

In October 1965, two days after I was shot down northeast of Hanoi, I arrived at Hoa Lo Prison—the infamous "Hanoi Hilton," so nicknamed by U.S. prisoners of war.

Hoa Lo Prison (nicknamed "The Hanoi Hilton"). Built by the French during the colonial period to hold Vietnamese political prisoners. *From a visitor's brochure from the prison site*

A 1993 photo of Cell No. 2 in the "Heartbreak Hotel" cellblock at the Hoa Lo Prison. This was the first cell in which Porter was held. *Courtesy of Will Furman Photography*

I was put in a small, filthy cell, and it was certainly the worst place I had ever been in my life. The smell from the waste bucket was bad enough, but there was another, older smell that was much worse. I smelled the misery soaked into the walls, and I felt it radiate from the narrow concrete bunks. These were foreign smells and alien to me, like everything else I had experienced so far. Hoa Lo had been built by the French to hold Vietnamese political prisoners during the colonial period, and many had passed through this very cell, leaving the bitter scent of misery behind. Perhaps one who had occupied this cell was now determining my fate.

The bottom photo on the facing page was taken in 1993, and shows the modifications made to the cell since 1965, when it had been occupied by American POWs. The wooden parts of the stocks were gone, the viewing ports had been covered over, and the underside of the slab beds had been blocked off.

The cell was in a cellblock that Americans called "Heartbreak Hotel," and I found it totally appropriate. I was there for about two weeks. The Heartbreak block had eight small cells: cell No. 8 was used solely for emptying night buckets and washing dishes, while the remaining cells were occupied by Dave Wheat in Cell No. 1; me in No. 2; Jim Stockdale in No. 3; Duffy Hutton in No. 4; Jim Bell in No. 5; Ralph Gaither in No. 6; and Rod Knutson in No. 7. Four cells faced the other four across a center passage, with the entrance to the block framed by cells No. 1 and No. 8. All of us except for Stockdale were from the *Independence*. Jim

Bell and Duffy Hutton had flown an RA-5C Vigilante and were shot down the day before I was while they were on a photo reconnaissance mission. Ralph, Rod, and I were in VF-84, and Dave was in VF-41, the other F-4B squadron on the *Independence*. October 16 and 17 were the worst days of the war for that ship. She lost four aircraft: two pilots were KIA (killed in action) and six were captured.

Each Heartbreak cell was made up of two concrete slabs with a narrow space between them. Each slab had built-in leg-irons that could be locked and unlocked with a metal tongue that ran through the wall and could be operated from the passageway. There was

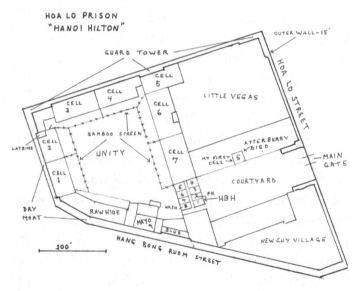

Floor plan of Hoa Lo Prison, including cellblocks that prisoners nicknamed "Little Vegas," "New Guy Village," "Heartbreak Hotel," "Camp Unity," and "Rawhide." *Sketch done by author*

also a viewing port at the end of the slab that widened pyramid-like through the wall so a guard could view most of the cell from the outside.

During those two weeks in Cell No. 2, I spent hours each day in interrogations, usually followed by additional time in the leg-irons as punishment for my "bad attitude." We could talk to each other if the guards weren't around. Dave Wheat was our lookout. A whistled "Pop Goes the Weasel" was the danger signal, and "Mary Had a Little Lamb" was the all clear.

I used the built-in stocks for a pillow when my feet were not locked in them, which occurred relatively rarely. So far, there was nothing I could not endure—the stocks, the beatings, the lack of sufficient food or water, the constant yelling by the guards that I was a criminal and had no rights, rank, or status at all—but I had a feeling that things could get much worse, and they did.

I frequently found myself in the quiz room just behind Heartbreak, sitting across from the interrogator, whom we called The Rabbit, and staring at the red star insignia on his cap. At this point it was still a game: he asked questions, and I answered with my name, rank, service number, and date of birth, as required by both the U.S. Code of Conduct and the Geneva Conventions of 1949.[1]

So far there had been little physical violence apart from slaps and punches, but there were always lots of threats. So far, so good. Now, however, The Rabbit was tired of the game. A guard was stationed behind me, and each time I refused to answer a question he slapped or punched my head, sometimes cupping his hand and striking my ear. Painful as it was, it was less than I had expected. The Rabbit was a skillful interrogator and spoke English well, but in the long run his arrogance proved to be a weakness. None of the interrogators had ever been to the United States, and they did not really understand American humor, idioms, or customs. It was a weakness that we learned to exploit.

The Rabbit was the only interrogator I knew who was with us from beginning to end. He was asking me questions just after I was taken prisoner, in October 1965, and was sitting across from me at a table at Gia

"The Rabbit," the North Vietnamese officer who served as chief interrogator of U.S. POWs. Ignorant about American customs and language, he missed many prisoners' resistance efforts, but still was relentless in punishing what he called "bad behavior." *Public domain*

Lam Airport in February 1973, when I stepped across "the line" into American custody.

In one session, The Rabbit asked me if I wanted to write a letter to my family. It was a question I felt I could answer, since it was one of the things guaranteed by the Geneva Conventions. Of course, I knew that the North Vietnamese did not abide by the Geneva Conventions or any other international law, but it seemed important to press for my rights anyway.

The Rabbit asked to whom I would send the letter, and I told him it would go to my parents. (I concealed the fact that I was married—no wedding ring, wallet, or pictures.) Next, he wanted the address, so I said the letter should go through the International Red Cross, just as the Geneva Conventions stipulated. He countered that without providing an address, I wouldn't be permitted to write, so I didn't—for five more years. I still wonder whether that was the right decision. Would agreeing to provide my mother's address and then writing a letter have saved my family the grief of believing I was dead?[2] Had I not been so determined to shield my wife, Marty, and our infant daughter, Dabney, from any sort of threat from the communists, I might have. At this point, however, I was still trying to abide by the Code of Conduct to the letter.

Looking back, I believe that my training in Survival, Evasion, Resistance, Escape (SERE) school was more a negative than a positive. We were taught that we should be willing to die rather than give more than just our name, rank, service number, and date of birth, but everything was not black and white. In reality, adhering to the Code required leadership and evalua-tion in light of conditions, and they were not taught in the SERE course, nor were covert communication skills or what we came to call "second line of resistance," which teaches you how to act when you have to do something as a result of torture.

After about two weeks in Heartbreak, I was taken to an afternoon interrogation and was told that I had a choice to make. I could answer the questions and then be moved to a "Better Place," where I could be with my friends, write letters to my family, eat good food, and play games. Or I could continue to refuse and then be moved to a "Worse Place," where I would live in soli-tary confinement. I could hardly imagine a worse place than the one I was in, but this was not a hard decision, since I was determined never to give in for better treat-ment. The Code of Conduct was still my guide: name, rank, service number, and date of birth—that was it, nothing more. We were to learn later—painfully—that this was not possible, and that it actually was not required by the Code.

Prayer sustained me, but I never prayed for release from this hell—only for the strength and courage to get through it and for the well-being of my family. At this point the choice was easy. My prayers and the advice from other Americans in Heartbreak gave me strength and some confidence. I did not believe there actually was a Better Place, and I was not going to give them anything in any case. So I consistently chose the Worse Place. I certainly do not regret this decision.

Former USAF major Fred V. Cherry pays a return visit in 1993 to Cell No. 2 in Heartbreak Hotel. *Courtesy of Will Furman Photography*

I did not know at the time that another POW was moved into Cell No. 2 right after I moved out. Fred Cherry, a U.S. Air Force F-105 pilot, had been shot down just five days after I was, and we were to meet in a short while.

The truck arrived very late that night. I was to learn that all moves occurred late at night and that the sound of keys jingling outside the door was ominous and fearful. (The unknown has its own special dread.) As the blindfold and handcuffs went on, I only knew that I was off to the Worse Place. When they came off, I knew that I was there. In the blackness, my only sense was smell, but this time it was new and more familiar— the scent of wet concrete. Suddenly I was Fortunato, bricked up in a dusty wine cellar, never again to see the light of day.[3] No tortured voices cried out to me in this place, but the terror was surely there. (Actually, I was in The Zoo, a film production compound that

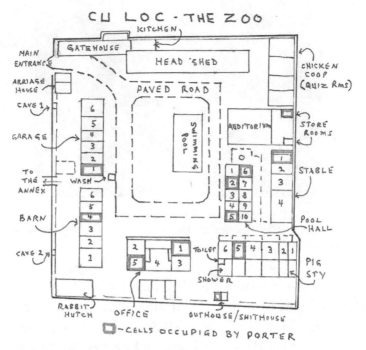

Floor plan of The Zoo, a prison compound in Hanoi. Prisoners were moved frequently from cell to cell, and the author was held in ten of the thirty-two cells at various times (marked in gray on the drawing). No reasons were given for the moves. *Sketch done by author*

had been converted into a prison, and this cell was in a building that we called The Office.)

I determined the dimensions of this new cell by feeling in the dark—hand over hand along the walls, beginning at the door until I arrived again at the door. It was large and empty, except for the few things I had brought—a sleeping mat, a cup, a thin cotton blanket, prison clothes, and a teapot and cup for water. There was also a rusty bucket in the corner.

I unrolled my mat in the cement dust and tried to sleep, but I could only think about what I no longer had. What had once been so close, my beautiful Marty and our baby daughter, Dabney, were now so distant and unattainable. I longed for the warmth of Marty's touch, the green of the trees, the smell of the sea—anything familiar and friendly.

Bones and muscles aching from my hard bed, I saw the early morning light seep under the door and over what was left. Then I understood about the concrete: the window had been bricked up all the way to within three inches of the top. Beyond the bricks were iron bars and then slatted shutters. I could just reach the opening with my fingers if I stretched.

The turnkey opened the door and motioned for me to pick up my "breakfast" of thin soup and a small piece of bread.

The interrogation involved the same crap as before: "What aircraft you fly? What ship you from? How many times you bomb our country?" And the same answers: "Porter Halyburton, lieutenant (jg), 677514, 16 January 1941." The same outrage: "knee down, hand up," and more blows to the head. "Think carefully, you blackest criminal, no one help you now."

After hours of this, I was back in the cell, exhausted and battered, but still with some tenuous feeling that so far it had not been as bad as I feared. I was still alive and I had not been hung up by my thumbs.

I knew that this was likely to get worse, however, and I prayed for strength and courage to endure what lay ahead. That evening I heard scratching at the window, and I could hear a breeze outside. Hoping to get a breath of fresh air, I chinned up to the small opening at the top of the window, and what I saw brought a surge of joy, amazement, and gratitude. There, thrust up through the slats of the shutter, was a green leaf—clearly a message from God, who had commanded the tree outside to deliver it by the only means possible. Somewhat reluctantly, I picked the leaf from the twig that held it out to me, and it became both a treasure and a source of strength and comfort. God had answered my prayer in a mysterious and wonderful way.

There was a moment of levity in the middle of this that also brought some relief from the misery and loneliness. One day, the turnkey opened the door for the morning cigarette—one of three we got almost every day—and handed me two sheets of paper and a small dish with a ball of rice. He made some hand gestures that I did not understand and then left. I thought, *Wow, this is great, some reading material and a little snack*. So I ate the rice as I read the papers. The reading material turned out to be "Camp Regulations," in English and Vietnamese, and then I realized that the rice ball was supposed to be used as glue to stick the papers to the wall. The turnkey was furious when he came back and saw that I had eaten the glue. He slapped me around a little, but returned with more rice and closely supervised the mounting of the regulations. He must have thought that I was the dumbest person in the world and probably had a good laugh with the other turnkeys, guards, and interrogators, but this fit in with my plans to appear young, dumb, and of little value in interrogation. I had a good laugh about it myself.

The interrogation continued every day, and was no laughing matter. Things got worse when I was presented with the evidence they had found in my flight gear. In our squadron, we tried very hard to remove everything that could identify us as to aircraft, squadron, or ship, so all patches came off the flight suits. Squadron personnel had trimmed all identification from our maps and kneeboard cards, and scraped our squadron logos from our helmets. In addition, I did not carry a wallet and did not wear my wedding ring. I had only my Geneva Conventions card and dog tags. Unfortunately, the ship's crew that maintained the Mark 3C flotation gear attached to the flight vest had written *VF-84* on the inside, where it wasn't visible unless it had been detached from the vest, which the North Vietnamese already had done and noted. Now, from that one little piece of information, my captors knew a lot about me. Yet I still would not confirm it, since that would have violated the Code. The one bright spot in this Worse Place was that Cdr. Jeremiah Denton, from my ship, was in the next cell, but that is another story.

More interrogation and the same old threat: cooperate or we will move you to a much worse place. Soon enough the threat became a reality, and I was awakened in the middle of the night and blindfolded. With my meager bedroll under one arm, I was led barefoot across the prison to the back of a large building that I knew was called The Auditorium.

My newest cell was a dirty storage room in the back, up a few steps from the large central room, previously used by the film studio for viewing films. It had no light, but the window had not been bricked up, although it did have bars and tight-fitting shutters. Again, I had to feel my way around the cell, and I found that it was quite small. I tapped on the wall opposite the window, but got no response. I realized that I was not only alone, but also isolated from the other prisoners. Before finally going to sleep on the cold cement floor, I prayed for a long time and asked for strength to endure what was to come. It was the uncertainty of what lay in the future that was so hard to deal with. However, I had my leaf and I had faith that neither God nor my country was going to abandon me in this place.

In the morning as the wake-up gong sounded, I awoke to dim light to see just how small and miserable my confines were. From the Vietnamese voices outside the window, I realized that I was close to the "head shed," which contained the interrogation rooms and administrative offices. How could I endure this proximity to my tormentors?[4]

About midmorning, the gloom was pierced by a beam of sunlight that came through a small crack in the shutters and struck the opposite wall with a sharp brilliance—surely a sign from God once again. Quickly I made a small paper cross from a scrap of what served as toilet paper and glued it to the wall with some rice grains at just the spot where the sun had struck. Each day, as the sunlight illuminated the little cross for a minute or two, I felt the presence of God, and it sustained me throughout that lonely and difficult time. Sometime later, that sunlight on the cross would sustain another prisoner as well. That's another story.

Aside from interrogation, the only time I got out of the cell was to take the honey bucket out to be emptied. The turnkey would motion for me to put it down between the two cellblocks—Pig Sty and Pool Hall—beside The Auditorium. I knew there were prisoners there because I could hear their soft coughs of greeting each time I carried out the bucket or picked it up after it had been emptied. Since the turnkey did not speak English, I would rattle off my name, rank, aircraft, and shoot-down date while pretending to ask the turnkey where he wanted me to put the bucket. I had already memorized the names of everyone I knew about—those in Heartbreak and the ones with whom they had made contact—so I assumed that everyone else also was keeping a list. As I was to learn later, not everyone listening to my identification litany heard it correctly.

Once again the interrogator gave me a choice: cooperate or go to an even-worse place. Once again, I chose. All the way across the prison next to the back wall was a small shed that had been used to store coal and some other things. We named it the Outhouse, or Shithouse. It was infested with ants, flies, mosquitoes, geckos, and, at night, rats. I finally was convinced that this was really the worst place they had. To begin with, the food was barely edible, and it was left outside the door for hours. When I finally got it, the meal was covered with ants. I was weak from diarrhea, sleepless nights, constant interrogation, humiliation, beatings, and loneliness throughout each day. After several weeks, I was very close to the end of my strength and resolve. The worst part was having no one to talk to, and my prayers were for strength and for companionship.

Another torment was what I could see through the crack in the door. There were Americans sweeping the walks, going to the washroom, perhaps heading for interrogation. Why was I being treated this way? Had everyone else answered the questions? Was I the only one holding out? What had others gone through to break them?

When the time came again to choose, I was not sure I could survive for long in *this* place, much less one worse than this, and I was tempted to try and get them off my back by answering a few questions. This was the hardest decision of all. I knew that to give in would be the ultimate disgrace and humiliation, something I could not do and could not live with, but I did not want to die, as I certainly would in a place worse than the one I was in. With great fear, I made the hardest decision of my life—and I chose the Worse Place again.

Surprisingly, however, my captors' idea of the worst place was not to make it physically worse; it was to put me in a cell with a black man. In their stereotyped view of Americans, they were sure that a young, Southern white boy would hate and look down upon all black people. This man was severely injured and could do little for himself, so when I was moved in with him in The Office and was ordered to care for him and be his servant, the tactic became obvious. He outranked me by two grades and was an Air Force pilot who had been shot down five days after me when his F-105 was hit while it was at a low level and moving at a high speed. The Vietnamese must have thought that forcing us together in this situation would set us against each other and break us both. That was not to be, despite the differences between us: I was young, he was older; I was junior, he was senior; I was Navy, he was Air Force; I was white, he was black; I was inexperienced, he was combat-seasoned; I was uninjured, he was severely injured.

Maj. Fred Cherry and I lived together for eight months, and the Vietnamese plan did not work. Instead of being the *worst* place, this had become the *best* place, for now I had a companion and something important to do. This gave meaning to my life beyond just survival and doing my duty. Caring for Fred helped me to put my captivity in a new perspective.[5] Now faced with Fred's severe physical condition, I no longer worried so much about my own problems and realized that survival meant so much more than just the physical. Fred nearly died several times during this period, but he was too determined and much too tough to die. He said later that I saved his life, but he was the one who probably saved mine. He was indeed a gift from God and the answer to my prayers. We became lifelong friends, and it was his example of courage, patriotism, devotion to duty, and personal integrity that set a high standard for me to try and maintain during the difficult years to come. The night we were moved apart, in July

1966, was one of the saddest of my life, and we were both sent back into solitary confinement and would endure serious torture to force our cooperation. It was strength from God, and what I had learned from Fred, that helped me get through that terrible time.[6]

The First Christmas

Fred and I lived together in The Office for nearly a month, freezing in our bare feet, thin pajamas, and cotton blankets. With longing eyes, I saw other prisoners who had shower shoes, and I thought that my being without any was part of the punishment.

Then one night we were bundled up and moved to another building that we learned later was called The Pool Hall. It faced the swimming pool in the center of the compound that, despite its outward appearance, was a filthy trash dump. Our cell was smaller, but nicer in some ways: it had raised platforms for bed boards, and a green-and-white tile floor, and it was a little lighter. The tile was cleaner, but colder, and there was no relief for our poor feet.

The next day was December 24 and the day after my second wedding anniversary. Early in the morning the turnkey arrived, and I heard him walk down in front of the cells, dropping something at the door of each one. Peeking under the door, I could see two pairs of rubber sandals and I said, "Fred, I think they just delivered our Christmas presents!"

They were not the store-bought shoes that I had seen on some prisoners, but rather what we were to call "Ho Chi Minhs"—made from old tires and inner tubes that the guards and turnkeys also wore. Ours, however, had no straps in the back, so we could not run in them. Our spirits rose a little along with the temperature in our feet.

Christmas morning came like any other day. The wake-up gong clanged us into wakefulness at 5 a.m. and we could hear the guards start their morning exercises with a cadence of *"mot, hai, ba, bon, mot, hai, ba, bon"* ("one, two, three, four"). Breakfast consisting of thin soup and rice hardly dented the hunger pangs as we talked of Christmas dinners with our families. At home, when I was growing up, my grandfather was the main cook in our household, and his food was always simple but delicious. We all did something, but I was pretty much limited to setting and clearing the table. Daddygran cooked the turkey with stuffing; Mom did the vegetables and baked bread; Nani, my grandmother, always made desserts, and my favorite was pecan pie.

As Fred and I talked about times past, I could picture that dining room in great detail with the Christmas tree glowing magically with colored lights and the four of us—my mom, grandparents, and I—sitting at the round table. The tree was right behind, where I always sat at the table.

Marty and I had spent our first Christmas together on our honeymoon in Key Biscayne, Florida. The honeymoon was memorable, but the Christmas part, not so much.

About midmorning the turnkey came and told us to put on our long pajamas, the usual signal that you were going for interrogation. This was the first time we had ever gone to interrogation together, so of course we already had our long pajamas on. To our surprise, the quiz room was decorated with a Christmas tree and colored lights. The tree was a Norfolk Island pine, and the lights were plain bulbs that had been painted. The Rabbit was all smiles and seemed quite proud of the decorations. He offered us a small cup of coffee with sweetened condensed milk, a little piece of hard candy, and a cigarette. Before taking them, I looked at Fred with a raised eyebrow as if to ask, "Is this a special favor, or will everyone get the same?" His slight nod told me it was okay to accept. The Rabbit tried making some small talk, but we just nodded and didn't say much. He pointed at the tree. "You can pray to your god," he said. We declined.

When we got back to our cell, we were feeling pretty good, since we interpreted all this to mean that the war was almost over, and we would be going home soon. As it turned out, there was a December "peace initiative," and I believe the Vietnamese thought something might come of it. We also thought that this was the reason for the talk of operating on Fred's shoulder.

"Fred," I said, "I don't have anything to give you for a Christmas present but this cigarette." He said, "Haly, all I have to give *you* is *this* cigarette." So we swapped cigarettes and felt something of the Christmas spirit.

As we smoked, we somehow got to talking about baseball and playing as kids in the local sandlots. Why that came up, I don't know because I really am not much of a baseball fan. Nevertheless, our companionship, that conversation, the shared memories, and those cigarettes made for a memorable Christmas.

Fred Cherry's Ordeal

When I moved in with Fred in late November 1965, he was in bad shape, and I was ordered to care for him, wait on him, and essentially do everything for him that he could not do himself.

Fred's most severe injury was to his shoulder. His arm had been almost ripped off when he blew away the canopy of his F-105 and it was swept into the six-hundred-mile-an-hour slipstream. A broken foot, his arm in a crude sling, and many cuts on his face made him a pitiful figure. I was simply overjoyed to see him, however. He was another American, no matter what color he was or what condition he was in.

Fred was suspicious of me at first, thinking that the Vietnamese had brought in a French agent to spy on him, so he did not say too much. After I tapped on the back wall to communicate with Rod Knutson and then explained to Fred how to use the Tap Code, he finally accepted me, and our friendship began.

After the succession of "worst places" that I had endured, I was in bad shape myself, but as the days passed, we both improved in health and spirits. Fred's shoulder and foot became less painful as the swelling went down, and I regained some strength with somewhat better food and a cleaner cell.

Like the other cells in The Pool Hall, Cell No. 2 had the window bricked up to within three inches of the top, with bars and shutters on the outside. There also were hooks on the walls for hanging mosquito nets. There were a few things the Vietnamese did that were both surprising and more humane than the rest of our treatment, and the most important was a mosquito net. Without it, our lives would have been even more miserable than they were, and the Vietnamese did not want us dying from malaria. They also gave us three cigarettes a day. Although in retrospect I wish they hadn't done that, those cigarettes added much to the day's activity and provided considerable enjoyment. We spent time anticipating their arrival, relished smoking each one, and critiqued its quality. Were there sticks in it? Did it go out? Did it fall apart? Was it a different brand? As soon as we finished smoking it, we looked forward to the next one.

I always thought the reason we got cigarettes was that Ho Chi Minh was a smoker and had spent time in prison, thus creating this small connection with us.

The day after Christmas we heard that the United States had halted its bombing of North Vietnam and President Johnson had launched a "peace initiative." We were optimistic and the Vietnamese seemed to be upbeat as well, and the treatment for most POWs improved somewhat. Still, nothing came of this initiative or any other U.S. attempt to negotiate with the North Vietnamese until 1973.

Sometime in mid-January 1966, an entourage of Vietnamese came to our cell and had a long discussion about Fred's shoulder. The camp commander, The Rabbit, the turnkey, and a couple of guys in white coats whom I took to be doctors all crowded in. The doctors traced lines on Fred's shoulder with their fingers in different places, and it was obvious to me that they were talking about surgery. They all returned after a couple of days and this time drew lines on his shoulder with a fountain pen. When they left, Fred told me his arm was not hurting very much and he could now move and use his hand and forearm a little bit. "Fred, do not let them operate on you if you can help it," I said. "I don't think they know what they are doing, and if they cut on you, you're bound to get infected. Just bear with it till we get home to get it fixed the right way."

At the time we were both optimistic that the war would be over before long, especially since The Rabbit had hinted that there was some sort of negotiation going on, perhaps because of the peace proposal that President Johnson had made.

On February 9, 1966, the Vietnamese came and took Fred away, and I knew they were going to operate on his shoulder. I was fearful that the operation would make things worse—that certainly proved to be true, and it was far worse than I had feared—but I was also hopeful that they were doing this to get him ready to go home because of the negotiations. Of course, the negotiations did not go anywhere, since the Vietnamese were firm in their position that the United States would have to withdraw from South Vietnam and stop bombing the North before there could be any kind of agreement.

The next day Fred was brought back to our cell in a body cast from his waist to his neck, with his left arm at a 90-degree angle to his body and bent another

90 degrees at the elbow. The plaster was still wet, and Fred was only semiconscious. He was put on the bed board with only the straw mat under him, and I was told to take care of him. I folded a blanket into quarters and managed to get it under him and used his clothes for a pillow, but it was totally inadequate. In the morning, he was awake and told me he was having a hard time breathing. I stuck my hand under the cast and found that there was only the thinnest layer of cotton between him and the bare plaster and that the cast was very tight. The first meal came, and I propped him up to feed him some soup, but he said the food only made the cast feel tighter, and he had more difficulty breathing. The only thing I could do to give him any relief was to grab his cast at the neck and waist and lift. This somehow eased the pressure of the cast, so I spent several hours each day holding him in this position. I also felt that he might get some relief if he was upright, so I got him up and we managed to walk around the cell for a few minutes, but he was too weak, and I concluded that that was not such a good idea.

I felt so helpless, and I knew he was not going to get better in this situation. The turnkey would not respond to my daily requests for the *bác sĩ* (a doctor, pronounced "boxie") to come. After about two weeks of this, with Fred getting weaker and weaker, he began to hallucinate and tell me wild stories about leaving the prison and flying one of the new (and not widely used yet) Convair B-58 bombers. He also described some little green men who came to work on his air-conditioning system every day, and how they scurried away to hide when the turnkey came. I knew then that he was badly infected, and this was confirmed when I lifted him by the cast and heard this awful slurping sound of the pus inside the cast.

I began yelling "*bao cao*" (report!) at the top of my lungs until the turnkey and a guard arrived to tell me to be quiet, but I persisted until an interrogator arrived and eventually the camp commander came in. I told them that Cherry would die if they did not remove the cast and give him antibiotics for the infection. I demonstrated the slurping of the pus, and they did bring some surgical scissors for me to cut away some of the cast. They all stood outside the cell while I did this, as Fred smelled terrible, but their reaction was dramatic when I managed to get a hole in the cast and about a pint of pus gushed out. I practically screamed at them, "If you do not help him, he will die."

Of course, I was beaten and once again made to go "knee down, hand up" (which meant to kneel on the concrete floor and hold your arms above your head) for my "bad attitude," but it was worth it. On March 12 we were moved across camp to The Garage, and then on the 18th Fred was taken away, and I desperately hoped that he was being taken to the hospital. I was hopeful he would return, since his mat and clothes were still in the cell. A few days later Fred returned on a stretcher and without the cast. I was shocked and dismayed at his condition. He was on an intravenous feeder, which I hoped contained antibiotics. In the morning, Fred told me that he was being squeezed by the stretcher. I discovered that the upper bar that keeps the stretcher rigid had not been locked, so Fred's own weight was causing the upper part of the stretcher to collapse. I could not get the bar closed, so I made a mound of our clothes and wedged it under his shoulders, lifting him away from the vise.

In the hospital the cast had been cut away, clipping his elbow in the process and revealing the gaping hole that had been his shoulder muscle as well as the many open sores caused by the tight cast. I eventually discovered nine open wounds on his emaciated body. The worst one, apart from his shoulder, was the gaping hole exposing his tailbone.

The most shocking thing was Fred's description of having been washed down with gasoline to wipe away the pus and dead skin. In his weakened condition he had passed out when the gasoline hit the open wounds, and this probably saved him from a great deal of additional agony.

The next morning the medic came, and we got Fred out of the stretcher and onto the bed board with as much padding as I could make from the blankets and clothes. He also removed the IV needle from Fred's arm and connected it to a tube that had been surgically inserted into his ankle while he was at the hospital. Shortly after the medic left, Fred said the pain was moving up his leg, and I knew that air bubbles were in the tube and that this could be life-threatening if they reached his heart. I yelled for the medic and immediately disconnected the IV, letting the fluid drip onto the floor and hoping the bubbles would not reach Fred's heart and kill him. The medic arrived with the turnkey and began shouting at me when he saw the disconnected IV, but I physically pushed him out the door and began yelling *bao cao*! until an interrogator came, followed by the camp commander. I was again beaten and chewed out for my bad attitude and my disrespect for the doctor and the guard, but I was so angry and fearful that Fred might die because of their primitive and careless medical care that I continued to express my bad attitude and disrespect to the camp commander, whom we called The Eagle. I told him that if Cherry were left in this cell and was not given proper care to stop the infection, heal his wounds, and provide decent food, he was going to die. I did not think they wanted Fred to die, and I had to convince The Eagle that he would die if they did not help him.

A different "doctor" came the next day and inserted another tube in Fred's other ankle, but neither of the tubes was ever used and eventually both of them were removed. Every time the bandage on Fred's shoulder was changed, it was re-done so tightly that the circulation in his arm was cut off so, each time, I had to undo the bandage and replace it correctly—at least I hoped it was correct.

Fred's wounds were not healing. He could not use his arms and could do nothing for himself. He was not gaining any weight, even though the food was a little better, and I was giving him as much of mine as he was able to eat. Still, he was not getting any better.

Finally, on April 10 he was taken away again, and this time he was gone for twenty-two days. All this time I was so lonely, and I worried that he had died. The turnkey and guards would not tell me anything about him, and I was even moved to another cell, which further increased my anxiety.

Fred received pretty good care in the hospital and was on the road to some recovery when the prison guards kidnapped him from the hospital and returned him to our cell. In the hospital he had been given a small inner tube to keep the sore on his tailbone off the mat when he was lying down, which was most of the time. He was returned to The Zoo in the back of a truck, and the inner tube had been punctured by a splinter in the vehicle's wooden bed. Since this was essential for Fred's healing, the guard agreed to patch it.

The next day, April 29, we were moved across the prison to The Stable, which was directly behind The Pool Hall and next to The Auditorium, which had been one of my "worst places." The Stable, as well as other buildings, had been screened off with bamboo mats, so the turnkey sometimes left the window shutters open so we could look out across the porch to a narrow strip of ground. One day the guards dug two holes there and planted banana trees, but they failed to water them. The trees quickly withered and died, of course, and I was sad to see them go, since they were the only living things we could see. "I think you are a lot like those banana trees," I said to Fred. "The Vietnamese go through the motions, but then fail to do the simplest thing to follow through." This sort of attitude was exemplified one day when the medic came in to give Fred a shot of antibiotics. He set up a little alcohol burner with a pot of water to boil the syringe and needle, just as he had been taught. When he tried to attach the needle to the syringe, he dropped it on the filthy floor. I expected him to put it back in the boiling water, but no, he put it right on the syringe. I tried to get him to sterilize it, but he said, "No, no, no!" He was the "doctor"—with the stethoscope and the dirty white coat—and he knew better than I.

On another occasion, he came to give Fred an IV. He tried to find a vein, but could not, so he just jabbed the needle in Fred's shoulder and left. As the shoulder began to swell up, I realized the fluid was just going in the muscle, not the bloodstream, so I pulled the needle out and let the fluid drain into the bucket.

Fred's tube sprung another leak and the guard again repaired it. One morning I heard an explosion in the cell, and I called out, "Fred, what was that?" "My tube blew up," he replied, in the most pitiful-sounding voice I had ever heard. This time the tube could not be repaired, and the Vietnamese would not give him another one. I made a doughnut out of my sweatshirt, and it served to keep his tailbone off the hard bed, but it was not as comfortable as the tube had been.

Through all of this, Fred had not bathed in months. I had given him sponge baths whenever I could, but I could not wash his hair, which was thick with a buildup of oil. I badgered the turnkey every day to let me take Fred to the bath area, and he finally relented. The Vietnamese had made this crude little enclosed shower shed with a stool, and this is where we were taken. The single light bulb was turned on by connecting two wires together with the little hooks on each bare wire just inches from the showerhead. As Fred sat naked on the stool, I began to wash his hair with the crude, homemade lye soap we were given. This just made a gooey mess and I had to rinse and wash his hair three or four times before I reached his scalp, but finally, it was done. A lot of his hair came out along with the goo. Bathing him was a new chapter in the story of our relationship and friendship, and it deepened the bond between us.

On June 29, 1966, the United States for the first time bombed fuel storage sites around Hanoi and Haiphong. We could hear the bombs and feel the earth shake as plaster pieces fell from the ceiling and the guards ran around frantically closing shutters. We were excited and hoped that this might bring the Vietnamese to the negotiating table. A couple of days later, the turnkey came around and collected a long-sleeved shirt from everyone in the cellblock, and then brought them back with three-digit numbers stenciled on the backs. There was a lot of speculation about what this meant, but we were not prepared for what followed on July 6. Trucks arrived in camp, and I was told to put on my shirt, but Fred was not. Blindfolded and handcuffed two by two, we were loaded into the trucks and taken to downtown Hanoi. I was cuffed to Art Burer, an Air Force captain. About fifty of us were marched through the streets of Hanoi on what came to be called "The Hanoi March." The march became a gauntlet that grew increasingly violent as the crowds lining the street began pelting us with stones, mud, sticks, shoes, and

American prisoners being paraded through the streets of Hanoi in June 1977, called the "Hanoi March" by American POWs. *U.S. Naval Institute photo archive*

spit, whipped into a frenzy by agitators along the way. The Rabbit was one of the inciters.

As the crowd became more excited, people pressed in close, and the guards could not keep them away. I was pelted with fists and sticks, and I was sure that someone would have a knife and it would slip through to end my life.

I believe that we escaped being slaughtered in the street by the mob by pushing our way into a nearby sports stadium. The gate was narrow, and the guards were able to keep most of the crowd outside. By this time, Art Burer and I had been soundly beaten up by the mob, as well as by the guards, who kept telling us to bow our heads and then hitting us when we didn't. The trucks finally arrived and took us back to The

Zoo. When I was locked back in my cell, I was relieved to see Fred there, but I saw the fresh blood seeping from the bandage on his shoulder, and I thought, *My God, I can't believe they took Fred on the march!* Fred looked at me and said, "Haly, what the hell happened to you?" I told him we had been marched through the streets of Hanoi and barely got back alive. He told me he had been to the hospital, where they had scraped the dead flesh from his shoulder without giving him an anesthetic. He confessed it was the worst pain he had ever felt, but he had endured it without crying out. He was still bleeding profusely and was very weak. I did what I could to stop the bleeding and prayed that he would not die. A grim terror descended upon our lives.

During that march through the streets of Hanoi, I looked at every camera I saw because there were foreign journalists in the crowd snapping pictures. At the same time, the guards constantly hit the back of my head to force it down in disgrace before the wrath of the people lining the street, who were also pounding us with rocks, mud, sticks, fists, and shoes. This was one of the few times during my captivity that I seriously feared for my life.

Months later, a POW who was shot down after the Hanoi March assured us that all fifty of the marchers had been identified, and Jerry Denton had told me that if anyone's photo had been taken in Vietnam the Central Intelligence Agency would have it. So, despite the terrible times that followed the Hanoi March, I felt confident that my family and my government knew that I was there. But I was wrong.[7]

A 2004 photo of Cdr. Porter Halyburton, USN, and Col. Fred V. Cherry, USAF. The two remained close friends throughout their lives. Colonel Cherry died of heart ailments in 2016 at a hospital in Washington, D.C. He was 87.

I was shocked by the brutality of the Hanoi March and by the things that had happened to all of us and to Fred, but at least we were back together. The next day I learned that many on the March had been brutalized through the night, tied to trees, and beaten. I was taken to interrogation and told that we would all be tried as war criminals and executed, but first I had to pay for my war crimes. Magoo, our sadistic turnkey, began beating me with a ferocity and anger that I had not experienced before. It was evident that things had changed dramatically.

We later learned that the Vietnamese had announced to the world that we were to be tried and executed for war crimes, thinking they would get great support from other nations because of the bombing of sacred Hanoi. What actually had been bombed was their petroleum, oil, and lubricant storage facilities and processing plants, and they all had been completely destroyed.

Fortunately, the plan to try us as war criminals backfired, and instead of support they got condemnation, even from some antiwar liberals on whom they had counted. President Johnson bluntly told the Vietnamese that if we were put on trial he would level Hanoi with B-52 bombing raids. There were no trials, but there were terrible times ahead for all of us.

On July 11, 1966, a guard entered our cell and gave me the "roll up your stuff in your mat" signal, which meant you were moving. As with previous moves involving Fred, I started getting his things together, but I was told that he was not going. My heart sank, and I knew that my time with Fred had come to an end. Perhaps the Vietnamese had finally figured out that forcing me to care for a black man was not the Worse Place that they had thought it would be—that perhaps they had an even Worse Place for me. And they certainly did.

As we said goodbye with tears in our eyes, I wondered what would happen to Fred without someone to care for him. I prayed that there would be another prisoner to take my place. I did not see Fred again until we were released more than six years later, but he was always on my mind and in my prayers.

That night they took away my best friend—a man who had demonstrated more courage, determination, and patriotism than anyone I had ever known. Throughout the terrible times that came, Fred was always an inspiration and a guide. I could not let him down.

The Briarpatch

After Fred and I were split up, I was moved out into the country to a prison that we called The Briarpatch. Some POWs were already there, and with the addition of the guys from The Zoo the prison was full. It consisted of nine small cellblocks in a tic-tac-toe arrangement, with walls enclosing the entire prison as well as each cellblock. We designated the cellblocks with letters A through I. Initially, I was put in Cellblock H, and my most vivid memory of that cell was being rudely awakened very early on the first morning by the crowing of a rooster directly under the window of my cell. Even though the window was barred and shuttered, the shock of this piercing alarm almost made my heart stop.

After a few days, I was moved to Block C, on the opposite corner of the prison. Six of the cellblocks had four small cells in a square. Mine was made even smaller by the excavation of a "foxhole" beside the built-in bed board. Some cells had two bed boards, but mine had only one. There was no electricity or running water, and the food was meager. I liked to think that, at some point, we ate the scrappy parts of that rooster that had greeted me that first morning.

There were ducks outside in the compound as well, and one day, when my window was left open, I witnessed the incredible harvesting of two ducks for the evening meal. Two guards herded the flock of about twenty birds into a corner of the compound and simply swung bamboo poles through the group until several were disabled enough for capture. Two of them were carried off, but others were left with broken wings and legs to hobble around helplessly. I thought to myself, *God, these people are not only cruel, but stupid as well!*

I was in Cell No. 3, which had common walls with 4 and 2. Red Berg was in No. 4, but it was almost impossible to tap with him because of the foxhole

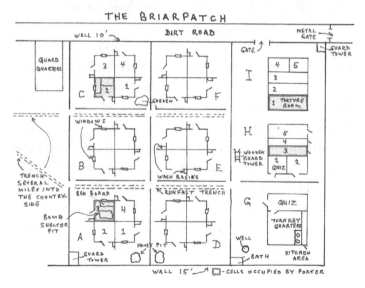

Floor plans of the Briarpatch prison in Hanoi show the cells that the author occupied (gray) during his time in this prison. The prison bordered on a trench leading to the countryside. *Sketch done by author*

next to that wall. Maj. Howie Dunn, an F-4 pilot, and Warrant Officer Freddie Frederick, his radar intercept officer, were in Cell No. 2, but I only tapped to Howie, since Freddie's hands were badly burned. (Years later he died of typhus.) Tapping was difficult, since our hands were either tied or handcuffed behind our backs during the day, so I had to back up to the knobby wall and tap very softly with the end of my finger, all the while watching and listening for any sign of a guard coming. This was very important because with our move to The Briarpatch there were several other changes that made our lives even more miserable. The most significant was the new policy regarding the prison guards' use of torture to get what they wanted and had not been able to get previously with threats, beatings, and isolation. Everyone at The Briarpatch underwent torture, but Howie was the only person I could talk to about it, and he was my senior ranking officer, which made it somewhat awkward. I was tortured three times—for three different "documents"—and the psychological pain of being broken was almost as bad as the physical pain, and it lasted much longer. It was only much later, after learning that everyone else who was tortured had been broken as well, that I recovered from those psychological effects myself.

Another terrifying threat loomed over us: there was a new punishment for communicating. Until now, being caught tapping or talking would result in a severe beating and a couple of weeks in leg-irons and handcuffs. Now it was made clear that communicating would result in two days of "heavy punishment"—i.e., torture—followed by sixty days in a foxhole, in leg-irons and handcuffs behind the back, getting out once a day to eat and use the bucket. Fortunately, I was never caught, even though I was always either the "comm guy" or a member of the communications team in every group of which I was a part.

We also had periodic drills that we called "run-fasts." By way of background, several times F-105s Air Force supersonic fighter-bombers had buzzed the prison and waggled their wings to say "hi," and the Vietnamese had come to fear that a rescue attempt might be imminent. The result was that we had to wear our long pajamas and handcuffs all day, so that we'd be prepared to be run out of the compound blindfolded and into a ditch that had been dug outside of the compound and continued for several miles. The "run-fast" was a drill to see how fast the Vietnamese could evacuate the prison in case of a rescue raid. Running blindfolded with hands behind our back and shower shoes on our feet was a real challenge. The guards added to the tension, yelling, "Run fast! Run fast!" at the top of their lungs.

Despite the danger of being caught, Howie and I tapped most every day, first about the torture and how best to resist. After the first time, we realized that we had to give them something, but our "second line of resistance" was to make that something unusable for propaganda purposes, since propaganda was more important to them than intelligence. We also compared our lists of names and told each other about our lives, both in the military and prior to that. As a Marine

Corps major and an F-4 pilot, Howie outranked me by two grades and had several years' more experience. Even so, he treated me as an equal, and over the course of several months we became fast friends. We even came up with a way to pass the time and keep our minds busy, especially at night in the dark with nothing to do: it involved menu planning. One day it would be Howie's turn to plan imaginary meals for the day and the next would be mine, giving us something to do at night. We had to be creative and come up with new dishes each day, so it became harder as time went on, but it kept our minds occupied.

One day I realized I had never seen Howie, so I asked him what he looked like. "Do you know John Wayne?" he asked. "—A lot like that," he went on. Since he was a Marine and a fighter pilot, I took him at his word and pictured him at about six feet, two inches tall, with broad shoulders, narrow hips, and rugged good looks. I melded that image with everything else I knew about him and carried it with me for the next five years. After we were moved, I was never in communication with him again and, since there were very few Marine POWs, no one with whom I lived knew him. I did tell lots of stories about our time at The Briarpatch—what a great guy Howie was, and how he helped me get through the worst period of my captivity.

Years later, in February 1973, as we were about to be released, the Vietnamese, having relaxed most of the camp regulations, allowed two groups of us, about forty in each of them, to come out into the big courtyard at Camp Unity (a section of Hoa Lo Prison) at the

Marine major John H. "Howie" Dunn and the author grew to be close friends during their captivity, but they got to know each other by tapping in code on their cell walls and never saw one another. The two met face-to-face just prior to their release, each surprised at how the other looked. *Courtesy of The Wall of Valor Project*

same time. I was talking to some friends whom I hadn't seen for some time when this stranger walked up to us—short, bald, and not very good-looking. He stuck out his hand and said simply, "Hi, I'm Howie Dunn." To say the least, I was stunned. "Howie, you son of a bitch, you lied to me!" I blurted out. "I know," Howie said, laughing, "but it was so much fun knowing the image you had of me all this time!" In that instant, he went from being a complete stranger to one of my best friends ever, and it was all due to a simple code transmitted with numbers one through five.

Locked Out at the Briarpatch

Life at The Briarpatch was tough in many ways. The fact that we ate both meager meals in the pitch-black dark deprived us of even the small pleasure of seeing what we were eating. It was always rice, but what came with it could only be determined by feel and taste. Rat turds were the worst, and they were hard to detect until they were in your mouth. Live cockroaches could usually be brushed off, but not always. Once I found a piece of wire in the soup and that was a blessing, since I could use the wire as a lock pick for the handcuffs. I got quite good at this and was never caught, since I could get the cuff back on; the turnkey rattled the lock on the cell door so loudly each time that it masked the sound of the ratchet re-engaging. Timing was everything.

In the early morning before dawn, the turnkey would arrive with a lantern or a flashlight to allow us to get the food delivered by the water girl. There was a small concrete basin just outside each room, so after we finished eating, we washed the dishes there, still in the dark. Occasionally the turnkey would allow me to wash out my shirt or shorts and I would hang them on the shutter to my window to dry during the day. I washed a shirt one morning and hung it on the shutter. When all that was done, I had to put on my long clothes and be handcuffed while it was still dark, and the turnkey moved to Howie's cell. Each of the doors to the four cells faced a different direction, so Howie and I might be out at the same time and yet not see each other. There was also a blindfold hanging on a nail by the door that we had to wear for the run-fasts. If there were no interrogations, we spent the day sweating in the heat with our long clothes on and little else to do besides tapping to each other and hoping not to get caught.

In the late evening, the turnkey appeared again with his flashlight and took off the cuffs, allowing us to get out of the long clothes and eat another meal in the dark. I finished washing my dishes when the turnkey was around the corner at Howie's cell, and, now more comfortably dressed in just shorts and flip-flops, I went around to my window to get the shirt that had dried during the day. As I came back around the corner, the turnkey was just locking my door, thinking that I was inside and not bothering to check with his flashlight. So, there I stood, facing a great dilemma. Should I seize this opportunity to try and escape or not? It only took a moment to conclude that I had no plan, no food or water, and nowhere to go in just shorts and shower shoes. So, I let the turnkey know that I was still outside, and he unlocked the door to let me back in. I spent the night thinking about this surreal experience and wondering if I had done the right thing. My chances of successfully escaping to freedom were just about zero, but the Code of Conduct said a POW must try to escape. The next day I tapped the whole story to Howie and asked if I had made the right decision. He said I had, but I still wonder to this day if I shouldn't have made the attempt, despite the near-certainty that it would have proven futile.

Several years later in The Zoo Annex, two guys, John Dramesi and Ed Atterberry, tried to escape, operating with much more careful planning, food and water, disguises, medicines, and other supplies. They went over the wall on a rainy Saturday night and were caught early the next morning. Both were tortured for days, and Atterberry was killed. The repercussions for everyone were severe, and others were tortured for weeks.

Our senior leadership had already concluded that even if we escaped from our prison compound we would still be prisoners of the country, and could easily be identified because of our physical appearance. The rule about escape was that you would not attempt it unless you had a way to communicate with friendly forces or a prearranged point of contact for rescue.

There were no successful escapes from North Vietnam.

Chop on the Log

Communicating with each other at The Briarpatch was difficult and very risky. The cells themselves made it difficult due to their configuration and to the foxholes that took up much of the floor space, which limited access to the walls. Punishments were terrifyingly harsh, but this did not deter us because it was so important to keep the comm net alive, even if it was just within the four-cell blocks.

As time passed, tapping became almost as natural as speaking or writing. The number combinations representing letters just flowed from my finger or knuckle in an automatic pattern, much as a skilled Morse code operator taps the key. The same was true when we received code: the letters and words, often represented by abbreviations, would just pop up in my consciousness without any need for translation. The letter R stood for are; U for you; V for Vietnamese; Q for Quiz (interrogation); T for the, those, them, or any T-word that worked in context, and so forth.

One morning, after breakfast, I suddenly began hearing a message in code. I knew it was not coming through the wall from Howie Dunn, the only person with whom I could tap, but it was there nevertheless. As the message continued, I realized it was coming from someone in the prison who was chopping wood. The cook shack occupied one square in the tic-tac-toe layout of the prison, and apparently some POW had been given the job of chopping wood for the fires, and he must have said to himself, "If you can tap on the wall, you can chop on the log." I never found out who that clever guy was, but his idea revolutionized the comm system. It meant that anytime you were outside doing a chore that made a noise you could send code, and the message went to everyone in the prison like a loudspeaker. There could even be a two-way comm using a kind of "Twenty Questions" method.

There were certain conventions that applied to any conversation, and these gave both flexibility and security. To make the "phone" ring (effectively signaling "I want to talk"), you tapped the beat to "Shave-and-a-Haircut," and, of course, the response (Hello) was "Two-Bits." "Two-Bits" was two taps, and it also meant "yes," "I agree," "I like that"—anything positive. One tap meant "no" or anything negative. Three taps meant "I don't know." A rapid series of taps meant "I did not get that. Please repeat." Two taps in response to what was being sent could also mean "Roger, I get it." This was useful when you were tapping a long word or idea and you got a "Roger" before you finished. It also encrypted the conversation in case the Vietnamese were listening in.

Sometimes the Vietnamese would come into an empty cell while the prisoner was at interrogation and would tap on the wall to see if they could get a response. If they did, the punishment was swift. If tapping did not start with a "Shave-and-a-Haircut," you did not respond. If you were outside you at least tried to transmit your initials so those prisoners looking through a crack or under the door could attach a name to a face.

So, "Twenty Questions" could go like this: a prisoner is seen being taken to a quiz and after an hour is dragged back to his cell in handcuffs. Another prisoner is taken out of his cell and ordered to sweep the courtyard with a stiff bamboo broom. He would sweep in code, beginning with FH (Fuck Ho) just to alert everyone that code was to follow. Then the message: HC R U OK (Harley Chapman, are you all right?). Chapman would respond with two coughs (meaning *yes*) or one cough (meaning *no*). From that point you could ask other *yes*-or-*no* questions. It was great fun to sweep in code while you were under the watchful eye of a guard who was pointing an AK-47 at you to be sure you did not communicate in any way.

At one point the Vietnamese were determined to isolate our most senior and stubborn leaders from the rest of the group and from each other. They put one of the prisoners in each of the seven cells in Heartbreak and stationed two guards outside to detect any tapping or talking. One of the prisoners decided to expand on the one- and two-cough responses, and the "Cough, Hack, Spit" code was devised. Coughs signified one or two, a hack (clearing of the throat) was three, a spit was four, and five could be either a sneeze or a fart. Once this was established, the guys did nothing but talk to each other for a good part of the day, and Heartbreak must have sounded like a tuberculosis ward. Even so, it didn't alert the guards because the Vietnamese themselves were always hacking and spitting.

We also realized that this simple five-number code could be used in many different situations anytime you could indicate numbers one to five. If a prisoner in an adjacent cellblock could see your door by looking through a crack or under his door, you could send code by sticking a piece of paper in and out under the door. If you could stand on a cellmate's shoulders and see out the vent port while others in a different cellblock were doing the same, you could "flash" code by passing your hand or a cup lid behind the vent. Tapping your foot, blinking your eyes, holding out fingers—all of these and other means could be used if others were watching you.

We also developed a one- and two-hand "Deaf-Mute" code for situations that enabled us to conduct two-way conversations using visual contact.

In addition to these primary methods, there were several specialized codes used in specific circumstances.

The "Slip-and-Slide" encryption code was used mostly in written communication by the senior officers

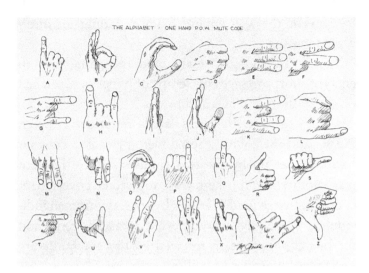

For situations where they could see each other, the POWs developed a "Deaf-Mute" code, using hand signals. *Reprinted by permission, from John M. McGrath,* Prisoner of War: Six Years in Hanoi *(Annapolis, MD: Naval Institute Press, 1975)*

THE TAP CODE

	1	2	3	4	5
1	A	B	C	D	E
2	F	G	H	I	J
3	L	M	N	O	P
4	Q	R	S	T	U
5	V	W	X	Y	Z

ROW #
THEN
COLUMN #

NUMBERS
SLOW

USE C FOR K

For years, POWs communicated by tapping in code on their cell walls. Here's how it worked. *Sketch done by author* to prevent the Vietnamese from decoding an intercepted message.

The "Tic-Tac-Toe" code used the game grid to encrypt short messages on scraps of paper or scratched on the bottom of plates and bowls.

There also were codes used in letters between POWs and their wives. Some were private codes that had been set up by the two spouses before the man was captured, and others were top-secret government codes that were used in letters by specially trained individuals. These guys were referred to as "mixers" and the bits of information received by this method were known as "martinis." I will say no more.

Communication was the lifeblood of our organization, and it was the most important weapon in our fight against the indoctrination and exploitation by the Vietnamese. If we were professional at anything there, it was communication.

Butts in the Back

Life at The Briarpatch was hard enough with the torture program, the run-fasts, handcuffs all day, no baths, crappy food, tiny cells, nothing to do, and no mail, but one day I found that there was yet another source of misery—the guards. The guards who patrolled the prison did not speak any English and were selected mostly for political loyalty to make sure that we could not corrupt them. There was only one guard at another prison who seemed susceptible to any sort of "corruption," and he did express in some way a desire to go to the United States. He was good-looking and usually wore sunglasses, so we called him Hollywood. Sometimes we got him to teach us Vietnamese words in exchange for English ones.

There was none of that at The Briarpatch, however, and the guards were always surly and stupid. One day the two idiot guards who had harvested the ducks with a bamboo pole opened the shutter on my window. They seemed unusually friendly that day and got me to come closer to the window, which I reluctantly did. This was a big mistake: one of them suddenly reached through the bars and got an arm around my neck. I was twisted around so my back was to the window, and the other one began pounding me in the back with the butt of his rifle. I knew I was in trouble when one of the hardest blows landed directly on my spine. As I collapsed from the pain, the other one released the hold around my neck, and I think they realized they had gone too far. They also made it very clear that if I told the interrogator about it, they would be back with worse punishment. I did not rat on them, but it was not out of fear. They left me alone after that, but I had back trouble for years.

A couple of weeks before that, in late August, another guard had opened my window and pointed at me and said "hot." Since I was handcuffed and in my long clothes with no ventilation, I was sweating profusely. I indicated to him that, yes, I was hot, thinking, *You dumb shit, what did you think I would be in this sweatbox?* He kept shaking his head no and pointing at me while saying "hot." Finally, he shook his head and went away after closing my shutter, and I was completely mystified as to what that was all about. Only later did I find out that my Vietnamese name was Hât, pronounced *hot* and meaning "sing" or "song." How they picked that name for me I do not know, since I never let them hear me sing. Perhaps it was because of the first syllable of my name. They gave all of us Vietnamese names and we gave all of them English names as well.

I Know Why Caged Tigers Pace

There were several other things that also helped me to get through this time, and one of them was exercise. From the very first day at Heartbreak, I made up my mind to try and stay as healthy as I could by eating everything and exercising as much as my physical space and diet would allow.

At Heartbreak, if I was not talking, eating, sleeping, or locked down, I was pacing on the slab—three steps from one end to the other, turn around, and three steps back, over and over. I estimated the length of one step and counted the steps so I had a rough idea of how far I walked each day. Sometimes it was several miles. I also did push-ups, sit-ups, and deep knee bends, but my main physical activity was pacing like a caged tiger.

Throughout my captivity, exercise was a very important part of each day, and walking back and forth in the cell created a bond between me and my caged tiger. The tiger paces because he wants to be free.

PRISON GARDEN

How long will the black roses bloom?
Perhaps for the day . . . or through the night,
But in the morning their thorns
Will be sharper still.

How long have the white roses bloomed?
They have long since died,
But left the fragrant memory
Of their passing.

When will the red roses bloom?
Perhaps tomorrow or tomorrow,
But I have tasted the bitter lemon,
Seen the deep purple,
Heard the rustling of the grass
And felt the tightening of her arms.

Stockdale

I had been in Heartbreak for about a week when we heard the sounds of a new prisoner arriving. The back of my cell and the other three on that side looked out into the entrance courtyard through the barred windows had been covered with wooden planks—so had the transom that faced the corridor between the two rows of cells.

I could see the courtyard through the cracks in the wood by standing on the edges of the concrete beds, and an American was being unloaded from an army truck. He had casts on his arm and leg and walked with crutches. As he was led into the cellblock, I could see him pass by my door by looking very carefully through the transom. He was put into Cell No. 3, right next to me.

When the guards left, Dave Wheat in Cell No. 1 signaled that it was clear to talk by whistling the first few notes of "Mary Had a Little Lamb." We soon learned that this new arrival was Cdr. James Bond Stockdale, and that he was the carrier air group commander on the USS *Oriskany* (CVA 34). Stockdale had been shot down in September 1965, and we were the first Americans with whom he had had contact. His shoulder and knee had been badly broken, and he had just been moved from a hospital. Although it was sad to see him in such a condition, it was some comfort to now have a senior officer among us junior officers.

As we talked, it became clear that Stockdale's injuries were severe, and he had doubts about his survival. He related the story of his ordeal over the past month with the thought that if he did not survive, perhaps one of us—who was younger and healthier—would be able to tell the story of his shootdown and what had happened to him since. It was clear that it was important to him that his family and the Navy know his fate if he did not return.

What I did not know at the time was his involvement with the August 1964 Gulf of Tonkin incident, which had widened America's involvement in Vietnam and had spurred Operation Rolling Thunder in the air war against North Vietnam. He had been the leader of the carrier aircraft launched against the North Vietnamese P-4 torpedo boats that had attacked the

USS *Maddox* (DD 731) on August 3, 1964. Again, on the next night, he was in the air in response to reports that the destroyers *Maddox* and USS *C. Turner Joy* (DD 951) were again under attack by North Vietnamese torpedo boats. Although the attack on the 3rd was real and the three P-4s had been pursued and attacked by Stockdale and his wingmen, there were no torpedo boats and no attack during the incident on the 4th—only confusion. Nevertheless, Johnson and McNamara had used this incident as the rationale for a retaliatory attack against the North Vietnamese city of Vinh on the 5th, in which Stockdale played a key role as a squadron commander. It was on this mission that Lt. (jg) Everett Alvarez was shot down and captured—the first POW in North Vietnam. Stockdale lived in fear that the Vietnamese would learn of his involvement and exploit it for propaganda. It seems that they never did make this connection.

Stockdale's A-4 Skyhawk, affectionately called a Scooter, had been shot down about fifty miles north of the port of Vinh on September 10, 1965. His left shoulder and leg had been severely broken when he ejected from the aircraft, and he was badly beaten by the villagers who captured him. That night he was taken to another village. Stockdale was on a small cot when a crazed man rushed in and tried to beat him with a stool. The villager was restrained, but later came back with a pistol and fired it point-blank at the commander. The shots went wild and hit the slats of the cot, bringing Stockdale down with it, but the bullets missed him entirely.

Later, the Vietnamese put casts on Stockdale's upper body and leg, and turned him over to some civilians, who drove him to the coast. At this point, Stockdale thought that the CIA must have known of his location, and that he was being taken to a rescue point. However, he feared that if the North Vietnamese spotted them while they were in the small boat, the civilians would dump the "evidence" overboard, and he would sink like a rock with the heavy cast on. He tried to tear off the cast on his upper body, and ultimately got rid of most of it, but the group headed to Hanoi, not Saigon, and they arrived at Hoa Lo Prison on September 12. Initially, Stockdale's physical condition was so bad that he was moved to a hospital, where he underwent several operations and acquired new casts. Then, on October 25, he was transported back to Hoa Lo and incarcerated at Heartbreak.

I was only at Heartbreak for a few more days and was moved to another prison—the first of the several "worse places" in which I would be put—but I carried Stockdale's account with me. At this point, we all realized how important it was to keep track of each other, since our captors were so determined that we would not communicate, not organize as a military unit, and not resist. I began to memorize and organize the names, services, ranks, aircraft, and dates of capture of everyone about whom I had heard. In the process, I discovered that I was the forty-first American to be captured—a number that turned out to be very important a year and a half later.[8]

Hanoi Chess

In early November 1965 I was moved to The Zoo and into Cell No. 5 of The Office. It was the middle of the night and pitch-black outside, and I had no idea what the place was like. While I was still in Heartbreak, Dave Wheat and I had figured out the Tap Code from a very cryptic glyph that had been scratched on the wall in the washroom, and we had practiced tapping some short messages through the wall. He was in Cell No. 1 and I was in No. 2, so we could talk when the guards were not around, but we figured there might be a time when the code would be the only way to communicate, given the camp regulations, which prohibited any communication or noise whatsoever.

So I was overjoyed to hear the "Shave-and-a-Haircut" call-up signal tapped on the wall from the next cell. I answered with the "Two-Bits" response and then heard nothing but meaningless taps after that. I finally realized that Dave and I had reversed the order of the taps designating the row and column in the five-by-five matrix that formed the code. It was laborious to relearn the taps (1–3 for C, 2–3 for H, 5–5 for Z, etc.), but I slowly picked it up and learned who it was on the other side. Jerry Denton had been an A-6 squadron commander on board my ship, the *Independence*, and he was shot down and captured in July 1965, three months before me, along with his bombardier-navigator, Bill Tschudy. I had a lot to tell Jerry Denton about what had been going on during the three months he had been a POW, and some of that was the sad loss of friends. He gave me a great deal of guidance and information about prison life, as well as the names of all the other POWs with whom he had come in contact. I gave him the names of everyone who had been in Heartbreak with me, including the six of us from the "Indy" plus Jim Stockdale. Jerry and Jim had been classmates at the U.S. Naval Academy, but Jim was senior by class rank. Thus began the list of names I memorized, which grew to 350 by the time the bombing in the North was halted in 1968.

After several days of this exchange of information, Jerry asked me if I knew how to play chess. I was not a great player, but I knew the moves and some of the simple gambits. He suggested that we each make a chessboard from the crude stuff we were given for toilet paper as well as pieces from whatever we could find. We were getting bread instead of rice at the time, so I decided to sacrifice some bread dough to make the pieces. It took a few days to make the thirty-two chessmen, and I used cigarette ash to color the black ones as well as the black squares on the board. Finally, we were ready to play, and each of us had a hiding place for his set when the guards came around. We opened up our boards and tapped the moves through the wall using standard nomenclature—KP to K4, QN to QB3, etc.—and this proved to be quite laborious, especially since we had to memorize the board after each move so we could hide the sets if a guard or turnkey came around. We did complete a few games; I think Jerry won them all. Not only did the games help relieve the boredom, but they brought us a great sense of defiance and accomplishment. Each day was pretty much the same: eat two meager meals, smoke three cigarettes, empty the bucket, and go to interrogation. In between, I was walking, doing calisthenics, tapping to Jerry, praying for strength and guidance, going over my list of names, and thinking about home.

One day I got word from Jerry that the Vietnamese had found a map in the cell occupied by Robbie Risner, and were beginning a thorough search of all the cells— which meant that we had better get rid of our chess sets. I tore up the board into normal-sized two-by-four-inch pieces and ate the chessmen. I had just finished the last of them when the Vietnamese arrived at my door for the inspection. That ended my chess-playing for quite a few years, but it was fun while it lasted. Soon after that I moved again.

Teaching the Tap Code

The Vietnamese had moved our group out to The Briarpatch in July 1966, after the Hanoi March, and the time we spent there was both interesting and miserable.

We came back from The Briarpatch in January 1967. I think the Vietnamese felt the place was too isolated, and therefore was a prime target for a rescue attempt. We knew they were very concerned about a possible rescue because the number of run-fast drills had increased. By January, they had seen several F-105s flying over the camp, low and slow, wagging their wings in greeting to us, so they must have felt the risk of an extraction was too great. By then I was in a different cell, Cellblock C, Cell No. 2, living with Paul Kari. When we moved back to Hanoi, Paul and I were joined by J. B. McKamey, living in Cell No. 5 of The Pig Sty in The Zoo. We had common walls with three other cells, but nobody was tapping on those walls despite our attempts to communicate. The guards there warned of the same brutal punishment as those at The Briarpatch had threatened for any violation of the camp regulations that prohibited communication or loud noises, but we finally got the guys on one side of us to respond to a "Shave-and-a-Haircut" tapping. It became obvious that the POWs there did not know our code at all. So, we began an extended and dangerous weeks-long attempt to teach it to them. We tried note-drops in the shower area, spoken bits as we passed by their doors, and actual tapping in code in the hope that they would figure it out. None of these worked, and sending Morse code through the wall was impossible. Then, one day I tried tapping twenty-six twice, and I got a tap in response. Then I tapped eight times and then nine times. The response was positive that they had received the message "Hi." So, then we used this rather cumbersome code to teach them the real code. It was worth the effort, since nothing was more important than getting everyone in the comm net.

Killed in Action

After I'd lived with J. B. and Paul for several months, they moved me in with Dick Ratzlaff, in Cell No. 5 of The Pool Hall in The Zoo. Dick was a radar inter-cept officer flying F-4s, just as I was. Cell No. 5 was on the end of The Pool Hall and was closest to The Pig Sty, the cellblock from which I had just moved. There was a crack in our wooden door that gave me a view of the outside and prisoners being taken from The Pig Sty to interrogation. I spent a lot of time at that crack gathering whatever intelligence I could, and it was always passed along through the walls to the others in the block. One day in February I was looking through the crack to see whatever there was to see, when an American walked by under guard, probably going to interrogation. I knew it was not someone in my memory bank of prisoners, but he did look familiar. Finally, it came to me: he was Al Carpenter, an A-4 pilot and a landing safety officer from the *Independence*. I knew he had not been shot down in 1965. Through our comm net, I sent a message to him, asking when he had been shot down. His reply, several days later, was terse: "I am so glad you are here and alive, because you were declared KIA."

The impact of that message hit me nearly as hard as the antiaircraft flak that had brought down my plane. I was stunned, and as many thoughts ran through my mind in a short period as had streamed by in the few seconds prior to my ejection. Had Marty remarried? Was my daughter still my daughter? Had I been forgotten? How the hell did this happen? Didn't they see me in the Hanoi March? What about all those photos?

Other messages from Al explained that he had been shot down on his second cruise to Vietnam and that he had been perhaps the closest to our plane on the day I was shot down. In fact, it was his testimony that he had seen no chutes and heard no radio transmissions prior to the plane exploding in a huge fireball upon impact with the karst ridge, and that resulted in the determination that we had not survived.

For some reason, Dick Ratzlaff was allowed to write and receive letters, while most of us were not. These were actual letters on full sheets of paper, not the six-line forms that we were to use many years later when the rest of us were allowed to write. So, in Dick's next letter, we constructed at least six identifiers pointing to me, including my identifier code (33); a Morse code message using the dots of the *i*'s and the dashes of the *t*'s; several code words that Marty would know came from me; and my mother's telephone number. I had been assured that the DIA, CIA, and naval intelligence would look at all letters from POWs for coded messages.

As bad luck would have it, about this time Dick's wife, who had been sharing his letters with the Office of Naval Intelligence, had grown disillusioned with the war, became an antiwar protester, and did not share this letter with the government. The thing that really got to me was the fact that she never even called the telephone number in the letter to find out what that was there for. My mother would have been thrilled to get that call and Marty, Dabney, the Navy, and the government would have known I was alive. She and Dick were divorced after the war, and I was never able to contact her to ask her why did she not do that simple thing? I have forgiven her, but it has taken a while.

There is a strange coincidence about this time in February. Marty found out that I was alive at almost the same time that I found out I had been declared

This is the way Cell No. 5 in The Pool Hall section of The Zoo looked when the author visited the prison complex in 1998, some fifteen years after release. He was held twice in this cell. It was the only one in the compound that had not been returned to its original (French colonial) state.

IN MEMORY OF
PORTER ALEXANDER HALYBURTON
LIEUTENANT JUNIOR GRADE, USNR
JAN. 16,   OCT. 16,
1941   1965
KILLED IN COMBAT OVER NORTH VIETNAM
SON OF KATHARINE PORTER HALYBURTON
HUSBAND OF MARTHA CARRELL DUERSON
FATHER OF DABNEY LORIMER HALYBURTON

Author's mother arranged for this tombstone when she heard that he had been killed in action in 1965, but the reports were in error, as the author lived to return to his family after his imprisonment ended in 1973. "I am glad to be able to look *down* on this tombstone rather than *up* at it!"

dead. It was Jim Stockdale who first got my name and several others out in a letter he wrote using "invisible-ink carbon paper" that had been smuggled in to him. He also included the fact that we were being tortured, and this was the first confirmation of this to our government.[9]

Pat Lamb

I first met Bob Purcell in the summer of 1967. Percy was an F-105 pilot and was, in my mind, the most outstanding of the mid-grade SROs and a most interesting and unusual character. I had heard stories about him, but my first contact with him was when we lived next to each other on the back side of The Pool Hall in The Zoo. I was still living with Dick Ratzlaff at the time, but we had been moved from Cell No. 5 to Cell No. 6 on the back of The Pool Hall. It was a miserable time, with intense August heat, no ventilation, little water, a cruel turnkey nicknamed Magoo, and heat rash over our entire bodies. Even the palms of my hands and the soles of my feet were dotted with little pockets of pus.

Cell No. 6 was on the back corner of the cellblock, and the sun baked the side brick wall in the morning and the front wall in the afternoon. Even the turnkeys had heat rash. It was the hottest cell in the building, perhaps in the whole camp. The mosquitos were intense as well, but the heat was worse—so much so that we often slept nearly naked on the concrete floor rather than on the bunks under mosquito nets. The bites were the lesser misery of the heat rash and the periodic attacks of itching that we called "The Siege."

The attacks occurred on our forearms and lower legs when we were eating hot food (we were given hot food in the summer and cold food in the winter) or when we tried to cool off with a little water. The itching was so intense that I was sure I would go insane if it lasted more than five minutes, but it usually subsided before that, aided by vigorous fanning.

The bright spot in all of this, however, was talking to Percy through the wall, which was no mean feat, but certainly was worth the effort and danger involved. We, of course, used the Tap Code for short messages, but for longer things, such as comparing our lists of names, we used "Doughnut Talk." This involved taking one of my thin cotton blankets and laying it out lengthways, then rolling it up into a long log. The log was then coiled into a doughnut shape, leaving a hole in the center about six inches in diameter. With Dick lying on the floor at the door and looking under it to warn for guards approaching, I would put the doughnut against the wall with my face pressed into it so that my lips just touched the wall. Once Percy was positioned on the other side of the wall with his tin cup against the wall at the same spot as my doughnut, I could begin talking right through the wall, with the cup acting like an ear trumpet. It was surprisingly clear. The doughnut also muffled the noise of our voices so they could not be heard outside the cell. Comparing lists of names was a lengthy and sweaty process, since I had more than 150 by this time and Percy had about the same. There were additions and corrections as we went through our lists, and one of the names I had lacked the additional information that we tried to include, such as shoot-down date, aircraft, service, rank, and physical condition. So, the name Pat Lamb had been a cipher for as long as I had it and I was anxious to find out more about him, although I knew he had been captured in 1965.

When we got to that name, Percy had a recollection. "I saw him back in November or December of 1965," he said, "and it was right here between The Pool Hall and The Stable, when he would come out from The Auditorium to bring his honey bucket to be emptied. I heard him say his name and I have always wanted to thank him because I moved into The Auditorium after he moved out and he had left this paper cross on the wall of the cell and the morning sun would shine through a tiny crack in the shutter and light it up every day. That was a powerful spiritual experience and real help to me at the time."

"Percy, what did this guy look like?" I asked.

"Well, he was sort of average height with shitty, fighter-pilot brown hair and not bad looking."

"Percy, that was me!"

So, I took "Pat Lamb" off the list, but I still smile every time I think of Pat Lamb and wonder how many others had that name on a list.

Percy in the Attic

Percy stories abound, but the one I remember and like the most happened in the same Pool Hall cellblock where I met him. We had a system for identifying cells by a numbering convention. Facing the cellblock (each one had a name), cells were numbered left to right on the front and then left to right on the backside, so The Pool Hall had five on the front and five on the back, with the front left corner being Cell No. 1. We called this prison The Zoo because the humans were inside and the animals were on the outside looking in. The compound had been a film studio used by the North Vietnamese army propaganda unit and was built in the French style with a swimming pool in the center (hence the nickname, The Pool Hall, for the building that was closest to it), trees and a paved roadway around it, providing access to the dozen or so buildings in the compound. From the outside, it looked to be a rather pleasant place. When it was converted for prison use, the French doors were replaced with heavy wooden ones with peepholes that could be opened from the outside. The windows were fitted with iron bars and bricked up to within three inches of the top—the only ventilation—and shutters on the outside. The Pool Hall originally had had three rooms, and these were divided into ten cells. The cells on the back side had no windows at all, and the only ventilation came from two three-inch holes near the ceiling and a small crack under the door.

This story about Percy had occurred before I knew him, and he was living in solitary confinement in Cell No. 1. The cell had two features that were important: it had no peephole in the door (we called them "flaps"), so the door had to be opened to see inside, and it had a hole in the ceiling. The hole had been cut when the building was converted for prison use, and it was done to provide access to the overhead to run electric wires to each of the ten cells. The remodelers punched holes in the ceilings and the wires dropped down with low-watt bulbs that burned during the night so the guards could check on us.

The access hole in the ceiling had not been closed or barred with barbed wire because there was no way to get up there. The ceiling was at least ten feet high and there was no furniture or anything to stand on. Another factor was a camp regulation that stated that any criminal who attempted to escape from the room would be severely punished. This meant torture and possibly death, and Ed Atterberry, one of the prisoners who *had* tried to escape, was tortured to death.

Percy learned through the Tap Code that the Vietnamese were starving several POWs at the other end of the building in an attempt to force them to cooperate. This was something new. Percy asked the senior ranking officer, Jerry Denton, for permission to try and help, saying that he had excess food that he did not want to go to waste. This was typical Percy humor. Permission was granted and he somehow figured out a way to reach the hole in the ceiling. He took the solid food from his small meal (bread with greens and a little pig fat) and used it to make pellets that he could put in his shirt pocket. He also rigged his teapot water jug with string from clothing. Getting up and into the hole was an amazing feat. Once in the overhead, he would pull the jug up with the string. At each cell, he would drop the food pellets down through the hole to the starving guys and pour some water that they caught in their cups.

Col. Robert B. "Percy" Purcell, USAF, was only a captain when he was a POW in North Vietnam, but he was a very effective leader in a number of situations when more senior officers were not present. His many exploits were legendary. *Courtesy of Suzanne Purcell*

Cell No. 1 in The Pool Hall at The Zoo. At the top is the hole in the ceiling that Bob Purcell used to get up into the overhead in order to feed the starving POWs in the building. The hinged parts are barely visible on the window at the right of the photo.

Percy did this every day for over two weeks and was never caught. During that time, he had only the thin broth to live on himself, since he fed his friends everything else. The Vietnamese must have been amazed at how long Americans could go without food or water, and that program was abandoned as a result. The story circulated around the prisons that Percy was willing to risk his life and health to help others—and that he was able to find a way to do the impossible—and it served as a great inspiration to all of us. We certainly learned that leadership did not come just from senior officers. I was privileged to live with Robert Purcell, under his command, and I learned much about leadership, courage, and compassion from him.

The last time I saw Percy before his tragic death in December 2009 was at the Naval Academy funeral four years before for Jim Stockdale, who had risen to the rank of vice admiral before he retired. We attended the memorial service at the Academy chapel and were walking together to the cemetery, and I asked Percy how he had been able to get up to the hole in the ceiling, since this was a question I often got after relating the story of this amazing act. Bob kind of grinned in his usual fashion, and shrugged it off. "Oh, I forgot," he said. This was typical Percy: he never tooted his own horn, but I think he really wanted folks to think he just leaped up there, Superman fashion, and this was not far from the truth.

In 1998, a group of thirteen ex-POWs went back to Vietnam on a tour, which included a visit to The Zoo, and I was able to see several of the cells that I had been

Thirteen former POWs pose at a reunion at Hoa Lo Prison in 1998. *Front row, left to right:* Capt. Irby D. Terrell Jr., USAF; Maj. Jack L. Van Loan, USAF; 1st Lt. Quoc Dat Nguyen, Republic of Vietnam Air Force; Capt. Harley P. Chapman, USMC; Lt. (jg) Wendell R. Alcorn, USN; Cdr. Fred A. Franke, USN; Lt. (jg) Porter A. Halyburton, USN. *Back row, left to right:* Capt. Thomas E. Norris, USAF; Lt. Robert J. Naughton, USN; Capt. Kenneth W. Cordier, USAF; Capt. Murphy Neal Jones, USAF; Lt. (jg) Lewis Irvin Williams, USN; Lt. Cdr. Render Crayton, USN.

held in, including Cell No. 1 of The Pool Hall. At the time, the Vietnamese Army propaganda unit was back in some of the buildings, and Cell No. 1 was an office of sorts, and there was an American in the room negotiating for film rights with a Vietnamese sitting across from him at a table. I excused myself and said that I needed to take some pictures but to carry on with their business. I photographed the hole in the ceiling as well as the window, so I was able to figure out how Percy had managed to get up there with only the things we had at the time. We had two thin cotton blankets, and our shorts and pajama bottoms had drawstrings in them. The window originally had shutters on the inside as well as the outside, and the inside ones had been removed when the windows were bricked up. However, the male parts of the hinges were still there, and this is what Percy must have used as an anchor for his sling. The sling was a blanket rolled up tightly lengthwise with a drawstring tied at each end so it could be attached to the hinge, making a loop. Percy used this loop as a springboard to launch himself to the opening with a running start from across the room. Hanging by his fingertips, he had to muscle himself up through the hole. It was an amazing feat, but that was Percy.

Part Two

———— ✺ ————

Surviving

The Onagers

CELL NO. 2 OF THE ZOO ANNEX WAS "HOME" FOR EIGHT of my friends and me for more than a year. Our desire to make the best of a bad situation—and an almost-magical mixture of personalities, experiences, and talents—shaped our lives together from the very beginning. It was the largest group of prisoners in which any of us had been, and we felt stronger and more confident amid our increased numbers.

It began in the spring of 1968, when Dick Ratzlaff and I were split up after having lived together for about a year in The Pool Hall in The Zoo. I usually had bad feelings about a move because it was hardly ever an improvement, and I always feared being sent back into solitary confinement. This time it was a good move, however, and my life changed dramatically for the better. Guys were being moved into the cell one by one and I was senior for a while until Glenn Daigle arrived and I became the unofficial executive officer. All of us in the group were the same rank—lieutenants (junior grade) for the Navy officers and first lieutenants for the Air Force—but we naturally had different dates of rank, which determined our seniority. I had been in prison the longest, so I was the Fucking Old Guy (FOG), which carried some status, and the others were Fucking New Guys (FNGs). Among the Navy guys, Irv Williams was an A-6 pilot and Mike Christian was his bombardier-navigator; Daigle was an RA-5 reconnaissance and attack navigator; and Fred Purrington flew A-4s. Tom Browning, Don Spoon, Gary Sigler, and Jack Davies all were Air Force officers. Tom Browning's father had spent nineteen months in Stalag 17 as a POW in World War II, so he seemed to be following a grim tradition. Actually, so was I, in a way, since Sgt. Edward Halyburton, a second cousin of mine once removed, was the first American soldier captured by the Germans in World War I.[1]

Although we were all about the same age and rank, and all of us were aircraft pilots or crewmembers with about the same knowledge and understanding of the war, we had very different personalities, which helped make this such an interesting group. We named ourselves The Onagers because someone knew that an Onager was a wild, stubborn ass found in Asia, and we felt that this was as appropriate a moniker as any. (An Onager also was a type of Roman siege engine.)

The Zoo Annex was separated from the Zoo by a wall, but it clearly was a part of the large complex that had been a propaganda movie studio for the North Vietnamese army before the entire complex was converted to a prison. The Annex was composed of five buildings, each with two rooms, that had been used for storage of film and photographic equipment—a mission that was obvious from the design of the buildings, each of which had double walls with air space between and a raised floor for insulation. All the rooms had had fans (since removed), as well as vents at floor-level for air circulation—much to our advantage because it made the rooms cooler in the sweltering summer and not as frigid in the winter. The buildings also had double doors, which gave us a bit more warning when the Vietnamese were about to enter. Each cell had its own courtyard, enclosed by woven bamboo panels about eight feet tall. In each courtyard was a well, a latrine sitting in a little shed

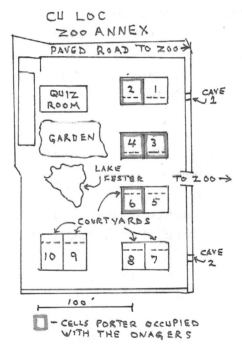

This floor plan shows the layout of The Zoo Annex, with gray borders outlining the cells in which the author was held. *Sketch done by author*

over a cistern, and a shelf to hold our chipped enamel dishes. We pulled water up with a bucket attached to a long strip of rubber, spiral-cut from an old tire. In the Annex compound, there was another small building, which was used for interrogation; a garden area; and a pond that we called "Lake Fester."

Into the wall separating the two prisons, the Vietnamese had built two tiny cells that were used for punishment. Too small to permit a person to stand up or stretch out, they were maximized for discomfort, and there was no ventilation at all. Being somewhat claustrophobic, I dreaded the thought of being put into one of them, but I never was.

Glenn Daigle was from Louisiana and proudly called himself a "Coonass." He didn't consider this an ethnic slur. He spoke Cajun French and was full of stories about Nutria Rats and Cajun food as well as his "Honey Babe"—his wife. We all called him "Coonass," which was even more appropriate because he frequently mooned us with two big raccoon-eye-like spots on the cheeks of his butt.

He often came out with colorful statements such as "It's always darkest right before it's [pause] totally black" and "He pulled up the *emer-gentsy* brake and come to a dead still."

Both of Glenn's arms had been badly broken when he ejected from his plane, and he had long scars on his upper arms from the surgery that the North Vietnamese had performed. His pilot had not shown up in the prison system. Glenn remained hopeful for years that the man might appear, but he never did.

One of my best Onager friends was Fred Purrington, an A-4 pilot, and we spent a lot of time together. Fred was a man of many talents and interests. He was an excellent golfer, and he played the drums in various jazz combos. Fred was from Dartmouth, Massachusetts, which is near a small town with the odd name of Padanaram (a modern-day version of a biblical name for Abraham's birthplace). South Dartmouth also was the home of the Concordia Company, which built the Concordia yawl, a forty-foot sailboat that Fred was in love with and vowed to own and sail one day.

Fred could describe the Concordia in great detail, and I became enamored with it as well, although I had never been sailing in my life. (Going to sea in an aircraft carrier does not count.) Fred also knew the waters around Massachusetts, all the small towns with picturesque harbors, and many of the surrounding islands. He and I would take wonderful imaginary sailing trips on our imaginary yawl, which we named *The Good Life* after hearing jazz singer Nancy Wilson sing that song over the camp radio one day. "The Voice of Vietnam" was a shortwave propaganda broadcast that the North Vietnamese aimed at GIs in the south. It carried lots of bad news about the war and protests in the United States, but occasionally it played American music to make the broadcast more appealing. Lots of Ella Fitzgerald songs hit the airwaves, but one day this Nancy Wilson performance really struck us for its beauty, images, and the dream of the good life to come.

For these dream trips Fred planned the route and all the places to stop that were interesting and had great restaurants, but I was in charge of all the food, entertainment, moods, and companionship. Marty went along on many of these, but not all of them, and I always provided an exotic date for Fred. The most memorable of his dates was Dominique Francon, one of the major characters in *The Fountainhead*, by Ayn Rand. The Dominique that I described for Fred was beautiful, of course, and had long black hair, green eyes, and a very sexy smile. She was almost as tall as Fred and wore a skimpy bikini most of the time onboard.

One night after we had finished the fabulous imaginary dinner I had prepared, the four of us were up on deck watching the sunset, with soft music playing, and enjoying the last of the Châteauneuf-du-Pape. In this romantic setting, I described how Dominique lay down beside Fred and rested her head on his chest with her hair spilling across him, but Fred only heard "hair on his chest" and practically yelled, "When did I get hair on my chest?" In fact, Fred did not have any hair on his chest, but this outburst completely ruined the romantic scene that I had so carefully built up. We had a great laugh over it.

Another wonderful character and my very good friend was Irv "Scurvy Irv" Williams. He won the push-up contest by a huge margin, doing 2,250 such exercises without a rest. (I, on the other hand, reached my personal goal of 100.) Irv had a fabulous memory as well, and remembered quite a lot of Spanish from college. What a joy it was for me to discover that he had memorized Garcia Lorca's poem in Spanish, "Canción de Jinete" (Cordoba), which I promptly memorized as well.

When the United States stopped bombing North Vietnam in 1968, I had the names of about 350 POWs memorized, most of them with capture date, aircraft type, rank, and service. I could recite the list of names alphabetically, by capture date, rank, and service, but the list changed periodically as we made additions and corrections. Irv had the lists as well, so we used each other as sounding boards for our daily recitations.

I never saw anyone enjoy a cigarette the way Irv did, except for Fred Cherry. Once we were given a deck of playing cards, Irv soon became my bridge partner. We even devised a new bidding system that was very successful. I didn't realize at the time that you must declare and explain the systems you use, so we were really cheating without realizing it.

Another guy I liked very much and spent a lot of time with was Mike Christian. He was Irv's bombardier -navigator in an A-6 and had been an enlisted man for a while. Mike played the guitar and was able to teach some of us to play, or at least how to finger the chords using our bamboo fans. The fans had a roughly semi-circular woven mat attached to a bamboo stick along one side. Using our homemade ink, we could color the six "strings" that ran parallel to the stick and the "frets" that were perpendicular to it. Mike could give us an idea of how a chord sounded by getting three or four guys to hum the individual notes together while one of us strummed the chord on the fan guitar.

Don Spoon could play the piano and, much like Mike and his guitar, he found a clever way to teach us chords on the piano. He lined up our toothbrushes and toothpaste tubes in a pattern that represented the black and white keys of a piano. He then showed us how to finger the chords, just like Mike did on his imaginary guitar.

Mike was married, with three daughters, and so was a source of information about parenting, since none of the rest of us had children except for me and I certainly had no parenting skills at all. Tom Browning had left a pregnant wife when he deployed, and she gave birth while he was a POW, but he did not learn for several years that it was a boy.

Most all the guys shot down after the Hanoi March in the summer of 1966 were subjected to torture as part of their "indoctrination" into the system. For some unknown reason, however, Mike Christian was not, and I believe he felt sort of left out and guilty about it. I always tried to be firm, but diplomatic with the interrogators, but Mike was usually hostile and let them know how much he hated them. As a result, he was often selected for the shitty jobs, like pulling the plug on the cistern below the latrine to empty it.

One time, for some act of overt defiance, he was taken away and tortured for several days. The night that Mike was finally returned to our cell is burned into my memory. We were all down and despondent over the fact that he was being hammered and were grateful when he finally returned.

When the door finally closed behind Mike and we crowded around him, someone said, "Mike, what happened to you? Where have you been?" I will never forget his answer: "I got tied up and couldn't get away," he said, with a slight grin on his face. Of course, we all knew what he meant: one of the methods of torture was what we called The Rope Trick—because ropes were used to contort you into impossible positions with joints all going the wrong way and circulation cut off. The fact that Mike made light of this terrible experience with this little bit of humor showed just what a hero he really was. It also demonstrated the power of humor when it is used in difficult situations.

Drawing shows one of the torture methods called the "Rope Trick" used by North Vietnamese. *Reprinted, by permission, from John M. McGrath,* Prisoner of War: Six Years in Hanoi *(Annapolis, MD: Naval Institute Press, 1975).*

Gary Sigler was another interesting guy, and he and I shared a love of science fiction. He told quite a few stories from sci-fi books that he had read, and even one story that he had written himself.

The Onagers were a diverse group, and often our discussions became heated over some issue, usually a belief. After a few of these, someone—I believe it was Mike Christian—suggested a way to minimize the conflicts.

The idea was simple. If you wanted your belief or position to be known but not discussed, you declared an IDV, or Individual Declaration of View. Someone else also could declare an IDV on that subject, but if he did, at least it did not usually lead to a divisive argument.

Since there were nine of us, we could now organize ourselves with assigned functions and duties for each man. Glenn Daigle was the skipper and I was the executive officer, but after that, the chain of command did not mean much. Everyone had at least one responsibility. I was the communications officer, a job that I held in almost every group of which I was a member. There also was an operations officer, a chaplain, education officer, entertainment officer, physical training officer, supply officer, sanitation officer, and security officer. Some guys held more than one job. The education and entertainment officers were especially important and very busy, since we had makeshift classes during the day and imaginary entertainment at night.

There also was a designated time for exercise—in the morning, before the turnkey did his count and let us out into the courtyard. That way we could rinse off the sweat from exercise and air out the cell. We also agreed on times for walking, since there was only the space in the middle of the cell for nine of us or however many wanted to walk at once. We walked in a race-track pattern and reversed the direction about every fifteen or twenty minutes.

Don Spoon was one of the very bright guys in our group, with a very analytical engineering mind, but he was never much on exercise. He and Jack Davies usually would be sitting on their mats while the rest of us paced.

Even though I only became especially good friends with three or four of the Onagers, I liked them all and they all contributed to making the sixteen months that we spent together the most memorable and tolerable of all the many situations I was in during my captivity.

One of the things that kept me going was music. Not that we heard a lot of music, apart from the occasional Ella Fitzgerald song that was mixed in with the propaganda broadcasts and the Vietnamese music that sounded so alien and hateful. I guess we hated it just because it was Vietnamese, or, more specifically, North Vietnamese. There was one instrument called the *đàn bầu* that we found particularly offensive. It was a one-stringed thing, very twangy, and we called it the "Swinette." We described it as "a hair from Ho Chi Minh's beard, stretched tightly across a pig's ass, plucked with the teeth." It is a hauntingly beautiful instrument when heard in the warmth of freedom, but it didn't sound that way in the cold cell of captivity.

I began to store music in my head right from the beginning and would work for hours recalling the words to songs that I liked and even some that I didn't. Since we were not permitted to sing or whistle out loud, I would make a kind of tunnel with my cupped hands from my mouth to my ear and sing softly to myself without the guards hearing it. At first, I worked on a group of Ray Charles songs, since they were fresh in my mind. My roommate on the Indy had a great reel-to-reel stereo, and our favorite tape was of Ray Charles doing "Born to Lose," "Makin' Whoopee," "Hit the Road, Jack," and others. Another one that seemed to stick in my head from the start was by a man named Nat Lucas, and the first line was like an endless tape playing over and over: "One of these days and it won't be long, you'll look for Nat Lucas, Nat Lucas be gone."

Before I moved in with The Onagers, most of my music activity was just recollection and preservation. This was 1968, and all these guys had been shot down at least a year after I had, so they knew songs that I had never heard.

I remember so clearly the first time I heard Mike Christian sing "Cryin' Time," by Nancy Sinatra. I was so entranced that I made him do it over and over until I had it memorized and could play it back in my mind any time I wanted. After that, I sucked his brain for every scrap of tune and lyric that he remembered, and filed them away, along with the growing mass of information pulled from all my new friends. I became a happy-music sponge, growing fatter by the day.

Mike was a Patsy Cline fan and knew most of her songs, and he was a country music lover in general. He spent hours happily strumming the chords to songs on his fan guitar while I watched and listened to the silent instrument. Very soon the warp and weft of my own fan seemed to produce that strange silent music that Mike had shared.

Fred Purrington was another music lover and a jazz fan. I learned a lot about jazz from him, but mainly about the musicians, the styles, the beats, and the tunes, since most of what Fred really liked was instrumental. My favorite vocalist was Billie Holiday, and I had already dredged up the lyrics to "Good Morning Heartache" and "God Bless the Child," plus the bits and pieces of a few others. I also knew most of Fats Waller's "Ain't Misbehavin'," as well as some songs sung by Nina Simone and Ella Fitzgerald.

THE MAN

The Man spoke to me
And I can still remember the words
That he said:
"Never fear that which lies
Beyond the scope of your imagination,
Never balk at that conception
Which seems to jump
Just outside your sphere of comprehension.
You are still young and not yet
Tempered by the fires of time;
You have not yet tested

The limits of endeavor,
Or know the reason for your being."
He said that "Although time may lift you
To the apex of your ambitions,
It will not be without great effort,
Nor should it be . . .
That man can live upon the blood
And sweat of his providers,
And never do or say
A worthwhile thing.
But you must be the Architect and Builder,
And claim the wealth
Of your creations."

The Escape

In 1968 there was an escape plan hatched in The Zoo Annex. I was in Cell No. 2 (The Onagers), and we got word that an escape committee had been formed, and a poll was taken to find out who would be willing to go. It became obvious that John Dramesi was the driving force behind it. Almost everyone else thought that although escape from the prison might be possible, escape from Hanoi and Vietnam was not.

Over the years there had been other escape committees—the Code of Conduct asserted that you "must make every effort to escape"—and the senior leadership had concluded that escape would only be possible from North Vietnam if one of two conditions existed. The first was that you'd have a means of communicating with friendly forces. The second was that you and your rescuers must have agreed on a prearranged pickup point. Escapes of opportunity were permitted, but not unless you'd managed to meet one of the two conditions.

By early 1969 it was decided that Dramesi and Ed Atterberry would be the ones to go, since they lived in the same cell, and everyone in The Annex would participate in the preparation for the escape. The Onagers were charged with gathering intelligence about the area just over the prison wall behind our cell. To do that, we somehow had to get up into the attic of the building to see over the wall.

There was a circular vent hole in the ceiling, but it had been sealed off with a lattice of barbed wire. Mike Christian and I became the work crew assigned to remove the barbed wire, and we took turns standing on the other's shoulders, using a stolen nail to loosen the wire. It took many days, many cuts, and aching backs to get it loose, but we finally did it, and we were able to get up into the attic to look over the wall. We reported to the escape committee that it looked like a good route for the breakout. We had been assured that Dramesi and Atterberry had met one of the two required conditions, but for security reasons we did not ask which one it was. Tragically, they had lied and had neither.

A rainy Saturday night was chosen as the best time to go, and that time came in mid-May. The message "Code Red" was sent, signaling that they had gone. They took with them all sorts of things that had been accumulated and stored in the attic of their building— food, water, medicine, and disguises to make them look more like Vietnamese peasants—but none of this helped them get out of the city, and they were captured quickly early that Sunday morning.

The North Vietnamese began their expected reign of torture with Dramesi and Atterberry. Ed Atterberry died from the torture—the most serious of the consequence of this rash and poorly thought-out attempt. Indeed, getting out of the prison compound was not the problem; that part of their escape was well planned. In fact, of the many prisons in which I was confined, only the Hanoi Hilton (Hoa Lo) was secure enough to prevent the escape of a determined prisoner. As the top U.S. commanders had warned, the real prison was outside the gates. In a country like North Vietnam, where do you go once you are "outside"? There were only two choices, and neither was good. You could try to make it to the coast, steal a boat, get out onto the Gulf of Tonkin, and hope the Navy would find you, or you could head west to Laos through dangerous jungles and try to contact friendly forces. If you fell into the hands of the communist Pathet Lao—which was highly likely—your situation would be far worse than it would be in North Vietnam. Of the many Americans shot down in Laos, only seven survived.

But the post-breakout punishment did not end there. In the aftermath of the escape attempt, one prisoner was taken from each cell in The Zoo Annex and from The Zoo itself. All were tortured in an effort to reveal other Americans' involvement in the escape. Red McDaniel was in The Zoo, but he was singled out for punishment because the code name for the operation was Code Red. In fact, he knew nothing about the escape at all.

Mike Christian was taken from our cell, probably because he was the most belligerent of us and did not hide his disdain for the Vietnamese. I remember when the door was opened late at night several days after the escape and Mike was told to roll up his few things in his mat—the signal that he was moving. I also remember the intense emotions I felt during those few minutes. The first was a huge sense of relief that I had not been selected to go because I knew how terrible it was going to be. The second was a pang of powerful guilt that Mike, my very dear friend, was going instead of me.

Over the coming weeks, we could hear the screams of men undergoing torture and we knew the Vietnamese would learn everything about the escape and punish those who were involved. We Onagers got our share of punishment for our part in the escape attempt, but it was nothing compared to what Mike and the others went through. In fact, most of our senior officers were in The Zoo next door, and their punishment lasted for months, even though most of them knew nothing of the escape plan.[2]

The Elf

When I moved to The Zoo Annex in April 1968 with the other eight guys, our lives changed in so many ways, mostly for the better, and the memories of all that we did during our time together still are vivid.

Moving to The Zoo Annex also meant acquiring a new interrogator and a new interrogation room. We called the newcomer The Elf because of his protruding and pointed ears. He was small, like most Vietnamese, and was not a bad sort at all compared to The Rabbit, Dum Dum, and The Eagle. The sessions with him were not so much interrogations as they were indoctrinations. I learned much about Vietnamese history, culture, and the prowess of the North Vietnamese and Viet Cong fighters, at least from his point of view. I learned that one such fighter could defeat a whole squad of Americans or a whole company of South Vietnamese. Though some of this was interesting, most was propaganda and exaggeration, so I constructed barriers to prevent its having any influence on me. To us, it was mostly lies and B.S.—or at least inflated by a factor of ten. So, if the news on Voice of Vietnam radio reported that they had shot down ten American aircraft, we knew they probably got one.

One big event that was celebrated and hammered into us was the shooting down of the three-thousandth American aircraft. Since this exceeded the entire inventory of U.S. aircraft of all types at the time, the air war should have been over when they reached this total, but of course it wasn't.

My tactic during an interrogation was to remove myself from that room mentally simply by concentrating on something else—a past event, dreams of the future, reciting poetry, etc. At the same time, I would stare at the star on the interrogator's cap or else at his ear rather than at his mouth. When I spoke to an interrogator, I looked him in the eye. When an interrogator spoke to me, I stared at his mouth. By observation, I found this was generally true of my conversations with other Vietnamese as well. I also learned that, by looking at something other than the other person's mouth, it caused a certain unease on the part of the questioner —a feeling that something was not quite right. Often it threw the interrogation off track. I knew it was working when The Elf moved his head slightly to get into my field of vision.

To keep The Elf from suspecting my inattention, I would give a slight nod every now and then. Occasionally he would ask me what I thought of what he had said, and I always replied, "That is very interesting." This worked well for a while but one day he asked what I thought, and I gave my usual answer only to be challenged to be more specific. When I could not tell him what he had been talking about, he frowned. "You have not been listening, have you?" he said. I confessed that I hadn't, and he got a very dejected look on his face and ordered me to return to my room, which I was most happy to do. That seemed to put an end to the "lessons."

The Elf's objective at the time was simply to engage me in conversation about almost anything. We all knew that carrying on a conversation with them was a slippery slope that would eventually lead to more serious and dangerous conversations. It was best to keep quiet or answer with as few words as possible.

The Elf's favorite ploy was to describe some "wise Vietnamese saying," such as "wet birds do not fly at night" or "the hand covers the handle of the sword" or "you cannot hide an elephant under a basket,"

and other gems of wisdom. After each of these sayings, he would ask if I knew any wise sayings from
America. I would always reply that we did not have
any. Nevertheless, he persisted, time after time.

About this time, we heard that the "reporters"
from the Voice of Vietnam and the *Vietnam Courier*
(a flimsy-paper, English-language news sheet) would
come to the prison periodically to hear what the interrogators had learned from us about American ways of
speaking, idioms, and humor. Once we heard about
this, we came up with a plan to introduce bogus information into their "system."

In the next quiz with The Elf, he quoted another
"wise saying" and again asked if I had remembered
any American ones. I changed my usual response to,
"Well, I do remember something my mother used to
say to me as a boy when something bad happened."
His face lit up with joy at this breakthrough and, as
he readied his pen and notebook, he said, "What was
that?" My reply was truthful—to a point: "It's an ill
wind that blows no one," I said.

So, we got on the comm net and asked everyone to
confirm this version if they were asked about it since
we suspected they would want verification. Of course,
they did, so this was obviously passed to the "reporters" and a few months later someone reported that
they had seen my version in the *Vietnam Courier*. I
regarded this as a small victory in our disinformation
program.

Glenn Daigle also had his own way of playing
tricks on an interrogator, and he told us how it worked

on The Elf. At any interrogation, you were seated on a very low stool in front of the Vietnamese, who sat on a much higher chair behind a table covered with a blue felt cloth. You were not allowed to cross your legs, fold your arms, or do anything "disrespectful." Glenn was quite tall, and his tactic was to begin by sitting very straight and then to begin slumping imperceptibly. He had found that the interrogator would often slump right along with him, apparently not realizing what was happening. When Glenn "got him on the table" he would suddenly straighten up, causing The Elf to also jerk up and wonder what had just happened.

First Package

I was with my Onager friends in The Zoo Annex on December 2, 1969, when I got my first package from home. The Vietnamese had removed almost all the contents of the package, which was a shoebox that originally held about 2.2 pounds, the amount allowed by the Geneva Conventions. The box was mostly empty, and what was left was a pair of red socks, a pack of chewing gum, and four wonderful, beautiful photographs of Dabney and Marty. Dabney looked to be about four in the pictures and was the most beautiful child in the world. I had last seen her when she was five days old, so to see her in these photos with Marty was just overwhelming. What I didn't know at the time was that Marty had sent her first package to me more than two years earlier, shortly after she found out that I was alive and a POW. In that package was a hand-knit green sweater. But that's another story.

Those pictures inspired me to write poems about both Dabney and Marty and really set me thinking about our future lives together. I did not know at the time that both of my grandparents, with whom I had grown up, were dead. So was my mother, who died not long after she found out that I was alive. After my return, I discovered among my mother's papers a very poignant story she had written on her yellow newsprint paper. She had been the Women's Editor at the *Charlotte Observer* and later worked at the Alumni Office at Davidson College. The story was allegorical

The first photo the author received of Marty and Dabney in 1969. Dabney is about four years old in this picture and was only five days old when the author had last seen her.

about the phases and events in her life, and these were described as entering and living in different rooms of her house. The last room was the room of death and sorrow, and it was the one of my death. In this story, there was no hint that she did not believe that I was dead, but a friend told me that she always thought I was still alive. I am still not sure about that. I knew that she had experienced some psychic things in the past and I felt all along that she would be the one to sense my presence in prison.

She told me once about a boy she dated before she met my father. Like most other boys that age, including my father, the youth had joined the Army during World War II. One day, on a certain date, she had a vision—not a dream, but a vision—of this boy being killed in an aircraft over Germany. She wrote down the date and the time of this vision and later asked the Army for information about him. The report she got back described the manner of his death, just as she had seen it at the exact time and date that she had recorded.

As much as I wanted to have psychic powers, I did not. Nevertheless, throughout my captivity, I did try to send psychic messages to my mother. As far as I know, I never succeeded.

THE THREE OF US

Yesterday on meeting you,
Hoping without knowing you,
Knowing without asking you,
Loving without telling you.

The young and misty two of us,
Sharing each the best of us,
Accepting too the worst of us,
And we so good for both of us.

And as for me the faulty one,
The wild and hungry needy one,
To spend my life in search of one,
And finding you the perfect one.

And so we shared our pastel days,
Our soft and glowing magic days,
And you with child within those days,
And then our few but perfect days.

Now two of you to wait for me,
To love, to hope, to pray for me,
And I still feel you part of me,
Though you and she so far from me.

The future still so bright for us,
For you, for me, for three of us,
And she the best of each of us,
Will fill the lives of both of us.

LYRICS: DABNEY'S LULLABY

Playtime is gone, your old friend the sun went home,
Sandman is comin,' won't be long.
Close your eyes, Daddy's got a kiss for you,
Dreamy baby, sleepy time is here.
Oooh, good night, Oooh, sleep tight,
Dreamy baby, sleep.

(1971–HANOI)

LYRICS: MY LITTLE GIRL

My little girl is so exciting,
My little girl, what a dream,
She's got a smile that's the most delighting
Wonderful smile that you've seen.

Take Trevi's fountain, the rock candy mountain,
Mix with a peppermint twist,
Roses and spices, a way that entices,
Something you can't resist.

My little girl is a song and a picture,
Someday she will be mine.

(1971–HANOI)

Memory Bridge

True to their nature, The Onagers decided to defy the camp regulations in yet another way. The regulations forbade any games, writing instruments, educational materials, as well as a host of other things that might have enabled us to expand our lives beyond the barest existence. When the groups got larger, of course, this was more difficult for them to enforce, and we grew bolder in our covert defiance.

The toilet paper that we were given was about as crude as could be and still be called paper. Aside from the quality, the quantity was very limited, so using it for anything other than its intended purpose was a rarity. Nevertheless, producing a deck of cards became a priority, and we began a conservation effort that enabled us to accumulate enough paper to do it. We glued several sheets together using rice glue and then, using a stolen razor blade, trimmed them to a uniform size of about two-by-three inches. We then marked each card with inks made of red brick dust and cigarette ashes mixed with pig fat. We made a special hiding place, and whenever the Vietnamese came around, we stashed the cards out of view.

The cards were used for solitaire, poker, and gin rummy, but almost everyone wanted to learn to play bridge. I was the only one in the group who played bridge, and I had learned from my mother, who was good enough to have master points. I'd played a lot in college and knew all the various conventions. One of us did not want to play bridge, so with the eight of us we were able to play a crude version of basic contract bridge.

Our hiding place for the cards was fairly secure, but one day a guard opened the door unexpectedly and we were too late getting the cards hidden away before he spotted them. An interrogator and the camp commander were summoned, and they all expressed great anger and indignation at our blatant violation of the camp regulations. These regulations demanded absolute obedience to anything that the guards and turnkeys demanded; absolute silence, with no communication with any other "criminal"; bowing respectfully to any Vietnamese we encountered; keeping the "room" clean and neat, and not bringing anything unauthorized into the "room." Technically, we had not violated the regulations, since we had not brought anything unauthorized into the cell (well, we did have a stolen razor blade that we'd used to trim the cards into rectangles), but this did not lessen the fury over our doing something—like a putting together a game—that prevented us from devoting full attention to "thinking about our crimes."

So, we were put in leg-irons and slapped around, while the guards searched the cell thoroughly for other contraband. The cards were torn up and the bits thrown in the honey bucket. On his departure, the interrogator said that we were strictly forbidden to play cards. This seemed to be rubbing salt in the wound, since our cards had been destroyed.

Even so, most of us took this as a challenge, and we set about making plans to put together another deck. Meantime, I suggested that we try to play bridge without the cards—a sort of memory bridge. The fact that there were nine of us was the only thing that made this possible. The one who did not play was assigned to be the "dealer," and his job was to divide the "cards" into four stacks of thirteen mentally. Once he had memorized them, he gave a stack to each of four "hands," who had to memorize the stacks. After this rather lengthy process was completed, the "hands" consulted with the four "players" who also had to familiarize themselves with the hands. The bidding began normally, although there were lots of whispers as the "players" consulted with the "hands." Once the bid was made, play proceeded quite slowly, with the dealer as the referee, verifying as to who had the card that was being played and who did not.

The whole effort was mostly an act of defiance, and it gave us something to do while we were locked in leg-irons. It also reinforced the idea that the Vietnamese could never fully imprison us if we exercised our free will to choose how to react to each challenge.

Nevertheless, the process was so laborious that we finally gave it up after the leg-irons came off, but it did prove the point that our captors could control many things, but not everything, no matter how hard they tried.

Telling Movies

Once our group of nine Onagers got organized enough to have classes and exercise, evening entertainment also became an organized activity. Naturally, there was an entertainment officer, whose responsibility was to discover what everyone else had to offer and then schedule them for the week. The most popular entertainment was the "telling" of movies because everyone had seen lots of movies and could remember a good deal from their favorites.

I enjoyed Fred Purrington's telling *The World in His Arms*, about a Portuguese sailor (Anthony Quinn) and a beautiful woman (Ann Blythe). I would hear him tell this same movie several more times as we moved around. Each time it was different and none of the versions was much like the real movie, but it was a credit to Fred that he could make it entertaining each time. I lived with Fred, off and on, for a period of almost four years—longer than I did with anyone else. We got to know each other well.

Movie-telling became a real art form and some, like Fred, could make up a story from the skimpiest plot or a couple of actors, and others could roll out a film scene by scene with uncanny accuracy.

Since your time to tell a movie was scheduled at least several days in advance, there was time to dredge up as much as you could from memory and plot it out as accurately as possible. There were other things scheduled for the evenings in addition to the movies, so your turn to perform only came up every couple of weeks.

You could also consult with others who had seen the movie you were going to tell, just to fill in as many details as possible. The movies were supposed to last at least an hour so sometimes you just had to make stuff up. Sex scenes were the most popular add-ins, no matter what the movie theme was. Imagine a redo of *Picnic* that was R-rated.

Over time, movie-telling also became a creative-writing exercise, and a few of us became quite good at taking a title, a couple of characters, a scene or two, and turning it into a full-length flick.

After I returned home, I made a point to see as many of these "told" movies as possible. There were a few movies that were nearly identical to the told versions, and it was like seeing them again in a theater. Others were quite different.

Dental Care in the Democratic Republic of Vietnam

One of the fortunate aspects of my captivity was that I did not need dental care at all. I had a few chipped teeth from biting down on the small white stones that frequently were included with the rice, but they were not a problem.

Besides all the other terrifying thoughts that went through my mind during my first two weeks of captivity, I worried that I was going to have to have an impacted wisdom tooth removed surgically because it had started erupting and was growing directly into the next molar. I had had one removed in college, and it was a horrible experience. When this one began erupting, in early October 1965, I went to the dentist on board the ship, and he said they would take it out on the way back home. Not making it for the trip back home, I arrived at the Hanoi Hilton in significant pain from the tooth and this terrifying thought that it was going to get a lot worse, and any dental care was quite unlikely. However, a sort of miracle occurred: the tooth stopped erupting, and the pain ceased for the entire time I was there. I had it removed by an oral surgeon when I got home, and he had a hard time believing my story of the "miracle."

There were others who were not as fortunate as I, and I heard the grim details about two of them. The first was a guy who had bitten down on one of those "rice rocks" and had broken off the side of a molar, exposing the root. In terrible pain, he reported this to the turnkey, and eventually he was taken to see the "dentist," who was a very small female with a big pair of pliers and a crude dental chair. She had to climb up on the chair to be able to get the pliers in his mouth and when she did, she used the molar next to the bad one as a fulcrum point to try and extract the tooth.

This was not successful, and, in the process, the good tooth was broken. The guy was taken back to his cell with two broken and very painful teeth. There was no Novocaine to dull the pain.

The second involved my friend Rod Knutson, when we were at The Briarpatch in 1966. He was living in solitary, as I was, and he developed a severely abscessed molar. His face was swollen like a basketball, with pus and blood everywhere, which made him very sick. He showed the tooth to a guard, and later the guard took him outside, tied his wrists and ankles to a straight-backed chair, and tried to pull the affected tooth with a pair of huge pliers. He ended up crushing the tooth with the pliers and not getting all the pieces of root out of his jaw, so it stayed infected for months. Eventually, a large piece of root caused a big, festering boil on his neck below the jaw. It finally ruptured, and lo and behold the piece of the tooth's root came out, and his neck eventually healed up. No fake dentist and no Novocaine. So much for dental care in the Democratic Republic of Vietnam.

Bamboo Slide Rule

Another project with Don Spoon and Mike Christian while we were in Cell No. 2 of The Zoo Annex was to make a "slide rule." This had two parts, one mathematical and the other physical. Not being math-proficient, but good with my hands, I did the physical part—making the slide rule, based on the math done by Don and Mike. Simple slide rules can perform multiplication and division. More complicated ones can do a lot more. We were into the simple. Don and Mike calculated the logarithmic relationships (Greek to me), and I translated these to the two strips of bamboo that we had extracted from the screening fence that surrounded our courtyard. First, I rubbed each stick on the concrete until one side was perfectly flat and smooth so that the two sticks would slide against each other perfectly. I had a stolen razor blade in my "survival kit," and I used it to incise marks on both sticks that corresponded to the numerical relationship of the logarithms. A little "ink" made from cigarette ashes and pig fat was used to highlight the marks. When the project was completed, we had a working slide rule that could easily and accurately perform multiplication and division.

I think we lost the slide rule in the move to Cell No. 6, but the sense of accomplishment was rewarding and long-lasting.

More Onagers

After the escape attempt, five of the Onagers (Glenn, Fred, Irv, Don, and me) were moved in with four others (Ed Davis, Rod Knutson, Bunny Talley, and Marty Neuens) into Cell No. 6. I was delighted to see Rod; I hadn't been in contact with him since 1965. We became great friends, and he had much to teach me, since he was a couple of years older and had been an enlisted Marine before going to Navy pre-flight school just ahead of me. I always thought that Rod was the best radar intercept officer in the squadron and that is why he was assigned to fly mostly with Ralph Gaither, the least-experienced pilot in the squadron, who joined about the same time I did. Rod was a very tough and meticulous guy, and perhaps the first POW to be tortured for belligerent behavior back in Heartbreak. Our backgrounds and personalities were very different, but I looked up to him and respected him a great deal.

During this time there were many interesting things that happened, and one of the oddest was the distribution of "tea cozies," or what we called "snake baskets." Our water containers were straight-sided Chinese teapots with the wire handle removed. This was the middle of the summer, and the last thing we needed was to keep the water hot. Nevertheless, the Vietnamese brought around these insulated baskets into which the teapots fit, together with a little red pillow to be sure the water stayed hot for a long time. In the winter, this would have been most welcome, but we could never figure out the logic of giving us these in the summer. As I've noted before, Vietnamese logic often was unfathomable. We tried to find a use for the snake baskets, but other than providing hiding places for wires, nails, razor blades, and scraps of paper, they just took up a lot of room.

Each morning the turnkey would unlock the double set of doors to let us out into our little courtyard. The turnkey was supposed to count us every morning, but often this was just a casual glance at us standing at the ends of our sleeping mats. One morning we all put our snake baskets on our heads and lined up as usual as the guard approached. He opened the door, looked at us, and turned to go, but suddenly realized what he had just seen and did the most classic double take, nearly falling off the step as he twisted around for another look. He tried very hard to keep a straight face but found it difficult to suppress a grin. Later that morning The Elf came around to scold us for being disrespectful and threatened to take away our snake baskets if we did not show a better attitude. The next day the guard came and looked in the baskets and saw that we were not keeping the teapots in them. We removed all the contraband and, sure enough, the turn-key came a few days later to take them away.

One day I was taken to interrogation and was given a box of watercolors and a few sheets of paper. I was told that this had been included in a package sent by my wife because I was an artist and needed something to do. I denied that I was an artist, but I was sent back to the cell with the paper and watercolors anyway and told to "paint pretty pictures." I did not do this, since I was sure this was just another ploy to get propaganda showing how well we were being treated. We did use the paper and the black color in the box for ink, which was very useful for several projects. The Vietnamese eventually took away the art supplies when they realized that I was never going to paint anything.

Deep Knee Bends

In July 1969, after The Onagers were moved to a new cell, the new group drew upon renewed energy and a wealth of additional experiences, knowledge, movies, and friendships.

While I was with this group, there was an athletic contest organized throughout The Zoo Annex. The competitions were for the greatest number of push-ups, sit-ups, and deep knee bends. Someone in another cell won the sit-up contest, doing 3,000 of them without stopping. We heard that his tailbone suffered greatly. Irv Williams easily won the push-up competition with 2,250, and I achieved my own personal best of 100, as I related before. Bunny Talley and I were left as the sole competitors for deep knee bends after all others had dropped out with fewer than 1,000. After we reached 1,000, we each upped the score by 500 until Bunny reached 5,000. The only time slot we had available to do that many was at night, after the doors were locked. The roving guards could only open the window at the back from the outside to check on us, so we would stay out of the view from the window while doing knee bends.

At this point, I tried to shut Bunny out by doing 6,000. He responded by doing 7,000. I was confident by then that I could do 10,000, but the problem was that doing more than 7,000 would take more time than we had from the door closing at night to opening the next morning. By this time staying up all night doing deep knee bends was getting tiresome, so I conceded victory to Bunny, and we finally got some rest.

YEARS

The years expend themselves upon the walls
With slow and steady cannonade,
Without a thought for those within
Who peer beneath the door.

Fish wrappers today are yesterday's dreams
And soon to be ashes and smoke,
And only a few are judiciously saved
To be wrappers and liners and smoke.

We speak in tomorrows and old yesterdays,
For today is a crystal of time.
Preceding another to follow the other
In monotonous rhythm and rhyme.

Christmas in Hanoi

Christmas in prison was always sad because we were not at home with our loved ones, but some of the most memorable Christmases of my life were spent there. Of course, the first was shared with Fred Cherry, and that simple exchange of cigarettes and the telling of stories about boyhood times playing baseball brought a modest feeling of joy and peace to us both.

Another memorable Christmas was with the Onagers in Cell No. 2 of The Zoo Annex. Some of us got packages during that first year that we were together, and it was the first communication that any of us had had from home. The packages could be up to a kilo (2.2 pounds), but what was left after the Vietnamese pilfered or withheld most of it was small indeed. The most wonderful things were photos of Marty and Dabney. In one package I got a pair of bright red socks and a pack of chewing gum. The socks were welcome and added some color to our drab environment. I shared the gum with others, but I managed to keep my piece of gum going for nearly a month until it disintegrated.

I also got a new "towel"—actually a large wash-cloth—from the Vietnamese, since mine had become threadbare over the years. It was dark green and perfect for a Christmas tree when it was draped into a cone shape and supported by a stick. Silver gum wrappers were used to make tiny balls for the tree as well as a star at the top, and the red socks became Christmas stockings hanging below the tree, which was placed on a platform below the window in the back of the cell. The window could be opened from the outside by the roving guards but, because the walls were double with an airspace between and quite thick, the guards could not see the tree and decorations below the window. We took it down during the day, but it was a magical sight during the night. We also drew names and exchanged imaginary "gifts" that were to be actual gifts after we got home. Once we were released, Mike Christian sent me a brass desk plaque mounted on a wooden stand, engraved with my name and the words: Dreams – Action – Reality. Rod Knutson gave me a gold-plated Zippo lighter with my name engraved on it, and Irv Williams sent me a personalized silver beer tankard with a glass bottom.

REFLECTIONS ON CAPTIVITY

How can I measure the loss
Of my dimensions . . .
As I lie, spread across
This crass expanse of time . . .
Bitter years, devoid of latitude
Or luster;

My duty days of trial
And decision
Are but pages turned
But pages not forgotten.

Those countless hours
Of aimless retrospection . . .
Regret, restraint and introspection;
The strange monotony of
Unrewarded hopes,
Unconquered hopes . . .
Amidst my unborn tears,
Have tempered the mettle
Of my structure
And filled the empty spaces
Of my soul.

Part Three

———— ∞∞ ————

Beating the System

A Change for the Better

IN SEPTEMBER 1969, AFTER HO CHI MINH DIED, the Vietnamese must have taken a critical look at what their policy governing the treatment of American POWs had accomplished toward achieving their strategic goals. I believe they kept most of us alive because we were valuable in at least two ways—as bargaining chips and as grist for the propaganda they spread to help turn American and worldwide opinion against the war. That is why they used torture—to force POWs to make statements against the war and to confess that they had committed "war crimes." The Hanoi March in 1966 was part of this campaign, but it had backfired. Yet, the failure of the North Vietnamese to produce the desired result did not deter them from continuing to use us in this way to influence public opinion against what they called "the blackest of criminals."

By 1970 it had become obvious, even to the North Vietnamese, that the use of torture and inhumane treatment in violation of the Geneva Conventions of 1949, which they had signed, was having the opposite effect upon public opinion. Americans could be against the war for any number of reasons, but most of them would not support a country that was torturing fellow Americans. It had become clear that North Vietnam was using torture and was violating the terms of the Geneva Agreements, which governed the way that prisoners of war should be treated. North Vietnam denied entry to the International Red Cross, and it refused to allow American billionaire Ross Perot to deliver a planeload of Christmas presents to us. Perot also had organized a trip for a group of journalists to visit the POW camps in South Vietnam and North Vietnam and report on the conditions. They, too, were not permitted to enter the country. The Vietnamese correctly concluded that their treatment of POWs and refusal to account for American servicemen who were missing in action had split the antiwar movement in the United States and had weakened it significantly.

The National League of Families, which had been organized by Sybil Stockdale, wife of Jim Stockdale, as a support group for wives and family members of POWs and MIAs (American soldiers who had been declared missing in action), had begun to apply pressure on the North Vietnamese to treat us better— and it, along with many other awareness efforts, was becoming increasingly influential. In Paris, where peace negotiations had been under way since 1968, letters and cards asking for better treatment of POWs and MIAs arrived by the truckloads on the doorsteps of the North Vietnamese and Viet Cong delegations. Many other organizations were also putting pressure on them. Millions of Americans were wearing POW/

MIA bracelets in support of the effort to pressure the North. By 1970, the impact—in the United States and worldwide—had become substantial.

Ho Chi Minh's death provided the North with an opportunity to try to repair the damage by revising its policy toward us, and the result was a significant improvement in treatment for most POWs. Camp Faith (known as Dan Hoi to the North Vietnamese) was the ultimate expression of this change. It was built just for American POWs, and it was very different from any other prison used before.

Camp Faith was made up of several compounds with cells, and each compound could hold about sixty

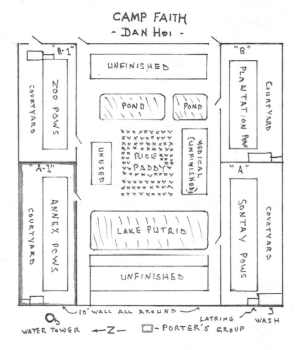

Floor plan of Dan Hoi Prison compound. *Sketch done by author*

POWs. We somehow found out that there were to be six of these compounds, arranged around a central area that had administrative spaces, a kitchen, guard rooms, fishponds, and interrogation rooms. The compounds were being filled as they were completed, and the first group to be moved there was from the prison at Son Tay, an ancient royal city about twenty miles west of Hanoi. The prisoners arrived sometime in July. Another group from The Zoo and The Plantation arrived in late July, and about 60 of us from The Zoo Annex were trucked in during August. The final group from The Zoo came in September. The other two compounds were never occupied, but if they had been the prison would have held all the American POWs—about 320 at that time.

Being at Camp Faith marked the first time that we felt we were being treated anywhere near the way the Geneva Conventions prescribed. The food there was much better and more plentiful, there were places to exercise and make coffee, play games, and bathe when we wanted to, and we received packages and letters that hadn't been pilfered very much. After a step-by-step process of gradual integration, we were permitted to gather in larger groups, and there was no torture or severe punishment.

Sang, Tang, Si, Con, Nat

The sixty of us from The Zoo Annex were in one compound of Camp Faith, which contained cells of eight or nine prisoners each. The guards could look into our cells from the barred windows on the outside, and one day one of them appeared at our window all smiles and began pointing at individuals, calling their Vietnamese names and giving the sign to put on long pajamas—a uniform we called "service dress seriously" because whenever we went to interrogation sessions the guards ordered us to "dress seriously." There were eight of us in the cell.

The five guys tapped for the interrogation were Bill Shankel, Bunny Talley, Jerry Singleton, Bert Campbell and Rod Knutson. The guard called out their Vietnamese names—Sang, Tang, Si, Con, and Nat—and there was a sort of rhythm to the way he spoke them. We looked at each other and someone repeated the sequence of names in the same rhythmic way, and someone else did the same until all of us were doing this little, sing song chant, over and over— "Sang. Tang. Si-Con-Nat"—with a pause between the first two and the last three run together. We even added a little dance step after a couple of times, and the guard clearly did not know what to think.

He stared with a puzzled look on his face and then began to smile, but caught himself, realizing that this was not an approved reaction for this sort of behavior. So, he put on a stern face and admonished, "No, no, no!" while shaking his finger at us. We realized we had pushed it about as far as we could get away with, so we stopped.

That little chant stayed with us for quite a while and was a great source of amusement.

The Son Tay Raid

On November 21, 1970, we heard gunfire and jet noise coming from somewhere close by, but had no idea what was happening. A few days later, without any warning, the guards came into our compound and told us to pack up. In a few hours, we were loaded into trucks for the ten-mile trip back to Hanoi and to Hoa Lo Prison, where our misery had begun.

This time we were packed into the large cells that surrounded the large central courtyard. During the time Americans had been held in Heartbreak, Little Vegas, and New Guy Village, these big cells had been used to hold Vietnamese political prisoners, who were moved to Camp Faith as we Americans moved out. Each big cell was filled by the prisoners from one of the Faith compounds. There were about sixty of us crammed like sardines into each of them. We did not know what had happened, but one of the cells still held Vietnamese for a few days, and some of them spoke French and some of us spoke French. It was from them we learned there had been a rescue attempt at the prison at Son Tay. They had heard that from the news broadcast over the prison loudspeakers. The raid was very successful except for the fact that there were no POWs there to rescue, since they had been moved to Camp Faith. I could not imagine how the Son Tay guys must have felt, knowing that they missed being rescued due to out-of-date intelligence. However, the elation that we felt, knowing that our government had tried to rescue us, was the most powerful morale booster imaginable.

The number of POWs in each of these large cells was reduced to about forty as the Vietnamese shuffled people around and tried to separate out the leaders they felt would be troublesome. Controlling groups this big was not something for which they were prepared, but they had been working toward it at Camp Faith, step by step. We were not used to it either, but it did not take us long to adapt. It was chaotic for a while: the POWs flexed their muscles as they found new strength in greater numbers. The Vietnamese tried to regain control and our senior leadership, now in good communication with each other and with us for the first time, tried to organize the rowdy prisoners and negotiate with the Vietnamese.

The most senior officers were put in a remote section of the prison to isolate them from the rest of us. We named this area Rawhide. Americans had never been held in the large cells in this part of the Hanoi Hilton, but now we were all in one place, and we called it Camp Unity. A well-organized command structure emerged over time, and we became known as the (self-styled) 4th Allied POW Wing. We called it the "4th" and "Allied" because there had been allied prisoners in World War I, World War II, and the Korean War, and there were a small number of Thai and South Vietnamese prisoners in our group.

Our lives were quite different from this point on.

Sleeping Bag

Despite the sweltering summers and hot falls and springs, it got quite cold in Hanoi during the winter. I occasionally found ice in my drinking cup in the morning, and more than a few times there was ice on the ground outside as well. Keeping warm was a challenge, especially with no heat and few clothes. When I was living with Paul Kari out at the Briarpatch in 1967, we even resorted to sleeping together, head to foot, to combine our thin, cotton blankets. It was a little warmer, but very uncomfortable. Lots of exercise during the day was essential for warmth, but at night it was difficult. Having cold feet at night—or touching someone else's—kept you awake.

After lots of experimentation, I finally came up with a pretty good solution—a sleeping bag made from everything I had. We were in the big Cell No. 2 in Camp Unity (the Hanoi Hilton), and sleeping mat-to-mat, so that helped some. But sleeping on top of one blanket and under another was not enough.

The bag construction worked this way: the first blanket was stretched out so that it would cover my head, with most of it off to the left side and the rest on the mat; the other blanket was stretched out on the mat, but with most of it off to the right and down so that it could be flipped up over the feet. When the whole thing eventually was folded over and flipped up, there would be three layers of the blanket over my feet. The right-side blanket would be folded over with enough room inside to slip my body in. Then all my clothes, including the ones I was wearing, would be arranged on top of that blanket with the sweatshirt placed where my torso would be. The left-side blanket was then folded over both the clothes and the other blanket, forming an insulated pocket for my body. The last step was to sit cross-legged on the end where my feet would be, with my feet tucked behind my knees, warming both my feet and the place in which they would be once I got into the rig.

Getting into the bag could be a bit tricky. After trial and error, I found that it was better to sleep naked or just wearing shorts, since the clothes provided better insulation between the blankets and my bare skin would cause less friction than my clothes did in getting in and out of the bag. It was always a rush in the morning to get out and put my clothes back on before I lost that heat.

Quack, Quack!

After things settled down in Cell No. 2 at Camp Unity, we organized into "flights" of about eight, and each flight had a flight leader, making it easier for the senior ranking officer to communicate with everyone through these six or seven flight leaders. My SRO was Al Lurie, an Air Force captain who I came to like and respect very much.

Later, Bob Purcell finally became the SRO, and this was about the best thing that could have happened, since he was a strong, courageous, and wise leader who knew how to get along with the Vietnamese without giving in. I had known him from our contact back in The Zoo. As a result, our cell probably had fewer scrapes with the turnkeys and guards than most other cells.

Communication between cells was set up very quickly, but this time it was not primarily by Tap Code or some variation, but by our Deaf-Mute Code, since visual contact was possible from one cell to the court-yards of adjacent cells. I was again the communications officer, and there were several memory bank POWs on the comm team to memorize any new information. A lot of official things came in from the Head Shed—that is, most of the seniors in the Rawhide section—but there was also news gleaned from letters from home and other sources. Lists of guys in each cell were updated as people were moved around, along with a healthy dose of humor.

Since we now had some paper, pens, and pencils we developed an "air mail" system where we bundled up the papers and threw them over the partition into the courtyard of the next cell when the coast was clear. Educational materials were delivered this way.

One of the funniest stories we passed around was about one of the guards patrolling The Moat, an area of about ten to twelve feet wide that surrounded the prison between the outer wall and the walls of the cells. At the end of our cell there was a latrine that was built on top of a cistern. There were several steps to get up to it and inside were two French-style holes with raised footpads. There was also a window that enabled you to look out on The Moat by hoisting yourself up using the bars in the window.

One day we heard a lot of quacking coming from The Moat, and when someone looked out he saw one of the guards holding a duck, plucking feathers out of its rear end. Perhaps he thought all that quacking might attract other guards, so he let it go after completing the plucking. A few days later the quacking started up again and someone rushed to the window and reported that the same guard had retrieved the duck, now nicely plucked clean in the strategic area, and had plugged in. Everyone lined up to get a turn at the window and witness this important and newsworthy event. I was one of the lucky ones to make it before Mike McGrath's turn. Until then, everyone had been very quiet so as not to interrupt the show, but Mike let out a loud whoop which, of course, *did* end the show, both for us and for the unfortunate "Duck Plucker/Fucker."

As a result, every time we would see the guard through the bamboo mats that formed the area of our courtyard, someone would let out a friendly *quack, quack!*—just to let him know what we knew.

The Chamber Pot Dance

We also used the latrine as a place to rinse off after exercise, since there was a big bucket of water and a white, enameled chamber pot used for "flushing" the toilet. I had learned to do handstands and eventually to walk on my hands, and this had become part of my daily exercise routine. I had worked up quite a sweat one morning and went to the latrine to rinse off after my workout. I was standing on the footpads, pouring water over my head with the chamber pot, when I lost my balance and started dancing around trying to recover. I still had the chamber pot in my hand, and it was bashing into the walls as I flailed around. I finally lost complete control and landed with a final crash. Everyone in the cell came rushing to see what was going on with all the racket and found me facedown on one of the concrete pads, with blood pouring from my face, still holding the chamber pot. I feared the worst, but all the blood was from incisions in my upper lip where the teeth had cut through. Once again, the Tooth Fairy had looked after me, and my front teeth were merely knocked loose, not broken.

The Jukebox

After I moved in with this much larger group of men, my days were filled with new and stimulating things. I quickly discovered the music men, and one of these was Phil Butler. Phil was an interesting guy, always busy with some project, doing his daily exercises, and happy to share his knowledge and ideas. Not everyone cared for Phil because he could be difficult and abrasive, but I liked him and admired him for his intellectual curiosity. Mike Christian and I had worked out a scheme for keeping track of all our individual interests (as well as the information that went along with each one), and this eventually became an alphabetical list of seventy-seven categories of interest for me. Phil organized his music into a "Jukebox." My own Jukebox quickly filled from the piles of 45-rpm and long-playing (LP) records, and tapes that I had memorized over the years. To that I added songs from Phil's collection. My favorite button was "C." As I organized it, C-1 through C-10 was the Johnny Cash section, C-11 through C-20 was for Patsy Cline, and C-21 through C-30 belonged to Ray Charles music. Punching the "P" button brought up the songs by Elvis Presley and the Platters, and D-1 brought up "Rattlesnake Mountain," by Jimmy Driftwood. The "I" button had lots of Burl Ives, and there was Little Richard, Chuck Berry, Bo Diddley, Ike and Tina Turner, Bill Haley and many other pre-Beatles rock-and-roll greats.

Later, I lived with guys shot down more recently, who knew songs from groups I had never heard of. "California Dreamin'," by The Mamas & The Papas, was one that I added to my Jukebox.

In 1971 and 1972 I began to put some of my poetry to music. I also wrote lyrics to music that I had composed. The first entry in the poem-to-song category was to Marty.

MARTY

How can I describe you
Or what you mean to me,
I cannot paint the picture
With the words for you to see,
My humble hands are useless
To translate this perfect thing,
I cannot capture sunlight
Or the beauty of the spring.

The bitterness and sorrow
Of years we've spent apart,
Have sealed the precious memory
Of our love within my heart.
I pray that time will never break
The bonds that hold us fast,
But more than time or memories,
I know our love will last.

In the morning when I wake
And find you by my side,
When once again together,
Tears of joy I cannot hide.
The music of your laughter,
The magic of your face,
No longer dreams but mine at last,
The warmth of your embrace.

How can I describe you
Or what you mean to me,
I cannot paint the picture
With the words for you to see,
But I can say "I love you"
In a thousand different ways,
Love you and adore you
To the end of all my days.

(1971–HANOI)

Sheet music for "Marty," a song the author wrote in tribute to his wife. The score was arranged by fellow POW Capt. James Q. "Quincy" Collins, USAF. The crumpled paper once covered a carton of North Vietnamese cigarettes. Paper was scarce for POWs.

Learning German

I remember as a child how fascinated I was by a sardonic feature in the *Saturday Evening Post* called "Tales Mein Grossfader Told," or "Fractured German," in which little stories were told in a mock German—one that used German-seeming words that could be understood by someone who spoke English but who did not comprehend German. I loved the way that German words often were made from two or more smaller words strung together in a long, descriptive strand.

I had taken two years of Spanish in college and didn't do very well. By the time I arrived in Hanoi, I remembered even less. Even so, I quickly became thirsty for any knowledge from my past and certainly for anything new.

When I moved in with Fred Cherry, I was overjoyed to find out that he had taken German in college, but I was disappointed to realize that he knew even less German than I did Spanish. I did pick up a few words, and that was enough to set me on a quest to learn more. For several years I did not make much progress, but then I moved in with The Onagers, and Mike Christian knew a little German, especially the drinking songs. Irv Williams remembered quite a lot of Spanish, so I began working on both languages, plus a little French. I found German noun declension and sentence structure difficult, but I loved everything else about the language.

Over time I learned enough German to teach a few beginner students in a small class. We met once a week in a small group and eventually tried to speak nothing but German to each other for an entire day.

We still did not have a dictionary or textbook, so there were always German words that we did not know. We solved that problem by making up fake words in German fashion. So, a duck became Der Schwimminquacken, and a rabbit was Der Hippenhopper. Words like these became part of my vocabulary without my thinking too much about it.

There were other classes being conducted around this same time in Spanish and French. Fortunately, by now the Vietnamese were lax about these activities and even gave us a small notebook. I was given the task of turning it into a trilingual dictionary, which was actually quadrilingual because it included English as well as French, German, and Spanish. English was in the first column, with the others to the right of it. We filled in the blank spaces as we learned more words, and we asked people in other cells to help. By the time I brought it home, the dictionary was impressive. In my cellblock it was used by all the language classes, but I was the custodian and editor.

After my release, living in Atlanta, I knew I wanted to go to graduate school, but I also understood that I probably should take a couple of undergraduate courses to get back into the swing of higher education. I told my adviser at Georgia State University that I wanted to take German in addition to a couple of other subjects. He asked about my prior experience and education and, when he learned of my Hanoi classes, he suggested that I take an equivalency test, which I did. I was as surprised as anyone when I passed German I and enrolled in German II. In that class, we often spoke only German and every now and then one of my Hanoi "words" would come hopping out of my mouth instinctively, even though I had since learned the correct words. Everyone in my Georgia State University class thought this was cool, and it became an informal game to see who could come up with the most clever new German-like words, and this took me right back to those "Tales Mein Grossfader Told" of my childhood.

Artificial Inspiration Generator

I lived with Mike Christian beginning with our time in Cell No. 2 of The Zoo Annex with The Onagers in 1968. After the escape, Mike was taken away and I did not see him again until we all came back from Camp Faith following the Son Tay Raid in November 1970, and the big group of us lived in Cell No. 2 of Camp Unity in the Hanoi Hilton.

Mike and I got along well, and I respected him for his up-front honesty, patriotism, and intellectual curiosity. We had done many things together in the Onager group of nine. We also shared a great love of music. I think it was Mike who got me interested in writing music, which enabled me to put a melody to one of my poems. I could write poetry based on our prison environment and my reaction to it, but it was more difficult to come up with ideas for song lyrics. So, Mike and I came up with a scheme that we called the Artificial Inspiration Generator.

We began by making lists of words in different categories—nouns of physical things; nouns of emotion; nouns of other non-physical things; verbs; adjectives; and adverbs. Then we divided the lists up into groups of twelve. We already had dice made from bread dough, and we used them to randomly select one or two words from each group. With those words in front of us, we would simply see what happened, what connections were made, what other images came to mind. If nothing happened, we would roll the dice again and get a new group of words. The first song I wrote using this device was called "Charcoal Heart."

SONG: CHARCOAL HEART

You've got a charcoal heart,
Black as the ace of spades,
But I can make ya stumble,
Bet ya take a tumble,
And fall into my arms.

You've got a one-way love,
You only know how to take,
But I know how to reach ya,
I'm the one to teach ya,
The music that two can make.

And you will learn the way
That love can play, a beautiful melody,
When I instruct the way to conduct
A two-part harmony.

I've got a torch for you
And charcoal burns so well,
Once I light the oven,
You're gonna be so lovin'
And give up your charcoal heart.

(1971–HANOI)

Survival Kit

Living in a large group of forty or fifty men as we did in Camp Unity had many advantages over being held in small groups or in solitary confinement. One of them was that it gave the prisoners a greater ability to collect, steal, or make contraband items and hide them from the turnkeys.

We used various techniques to distract the guards or turnkeys while we stole matches, razor blades, or whatever else we could. We were always on the alert to spot useful objects when out working or at a quiz and hiding them in a pants cuff or in our mouth.

At one point I had a "survival kit" that contained the following items:

—a nail with a sharpened and flattened point, useful for drilling or punching holes
—a piece of bent wire, to be used to unlock handcuffs
—a sewing needle made from a piece of copper wire
—a sewing needle made from a piece of bone. Both needles were shaped by rubbing on smooth concrete and eyes made with the nail drill.

The bone needle from the author's "survival kit" was the only item from it he was able to bring home.

—a paper package of purple ink powder, stolen at an interrogation session, mixed with water for ink
—several matches
—a small piece of mirror
—a stub of a pencil
—a razor blade
—a matchbox to hold everything

Hiding the matchbox was more of a challenge than stashing just a needle or piece of wire, but the Vietnamese did not search the cells very often, and I usually had the box wrapped up in my clothing. Sometimes, if we thought there might be a search, I would tie the box on the string belt of my shorts and hang it inside, since the Vietnamese were not likely to look there. I eventually lost most of the items (except for the two needles) to a search.

Boils, Bedbugs, and Pinkeye

Brutal treatment by the Vietnamese was not the only thing with which we had to contend. There were maladies caused by the unsanitary conditions, bad food, rats, and other vermin, heat in unventilated cells, and the inadequate clothing in the face of cold temperatures.

Out at The Briarpatch, in that tiny cell with only a bed board, bucket, and a bomb shelter, I developed a cold that was worse than any cold I had ever had. The flow of mucus was relentless, and I had nothing but my small hand-towel to use as a handkerchief. With no way to wash the handkerchief, the only thing I could do was drape it over the edge of the foxhole at night and let the ants clean it. In the morning it would still be stiff, but most of the mucus would be gone.

In the large cells in the Hanoi Hilton we were besieged by three plagues at various times—boils, bedbugs, and pinkeye. The Vietnamese did allow us to put our blankets and mats out in the sun to get rid of the bedbugs, but there was nothing to deal with the boils and the pinkeye.

We also suffered from an intestinal problem we called "Grun Luft" (Green Gas, since we were studying German at the time) because the diarrhea was green, and the gas came out both ends. The Vietnamese told us to wrap a blanket (bellyband) around our midsections to keep warm and occasionally brought us bland rice gruel, but that was the extent of our treatment, aside from the occasional small purple pill we called a "plug." We found it made good ink when dissolved in a little water.

Intestinal worms were a problem as well. Some guys had night crawlers, and most of us, including the Vietnamese, had pinworms. The Vietnamese did offer a yearly "worm cure," but most of us refused it when we found out that the so-called cure actually was arsenic. One time, when I was living at The Briarpatch with Paul Kari, I was able to steal a handful of very small but powerful hot peppers. It was on a very rare occasion when we got out to hoe weeds in the small garden in the compound, and I was able to hide the peppers by rolling them up in the cuffs of my pajamas. We crushed a few of them up in the soup each meal for several days, as hot as we could stand it, and this drove the worms out. It meant that I had to sit on the bucket for quite some time while they evacuated. The worms were not the only ones to feel the heat!

Of course, there was also jock itch and other fungal infections that plagued us.

The Russian Novel

For some reason that we never quite figured out, in March 1972 a bunch of us were moved from the big Cell No. 4 in Unity back to The Zoo, practically where I started from, in The Pool Hall.

The Vietnamese had configured the cells back to the original three, and I was in what was now Cell No. 3 with five or six others. I think this was the least favorite group that I ever was in, but the bright spot was that Bob Purcell was the SRO in one of the other cells and Fred Purrington was in there, too. We were locked in the cells at night, but they were open during most of the day and there was an enclosed courtyard made from bamboo mats. We were there for less than two months before going back to Camp Unity in the Hanoi Hilton.

One evening our turnkey arrived to lock everyone in the cells and he handed me a book. He said we could keep it overnight but had to pass it on to another group the next evening. As an English major and a fast reader, I was elected to read the book and then tell everyone else what it was about. I knew I would have to read all night to get through it and this was made even more difficult because the only light came from a bare, twenty-five-watt bulb hanging from the ceiling.

The book was an English translation of *History of a Town*, a Russian novel by Mikhail Saltykov-Shchedrin (1826–1889). Since I used my speed-reading skills to get through it in such a short time, I probably missed a lot of detail and characters' names, but I remembered enough to spend more than an hour the next night telling the story to the group. It was a satirical work about a town with the Russian name, Glupov, or "Foolsville" in English. I assumed it was a thinly veiled critique of the Tsarist Russian bureaucracy.

Seventy-Seven Categories

I was very fortunate to live with so many interesting, knowledgeable, and talented guys over the years of my imprisonment, and I learned so very much from them. Conversations with them or classes they led often sparked my interest in a new subject or activity. Over time I came up with a method of cataloging these interests so I could periodically go back, add new information, or review the old, so as not to forget.

The scheme was a mental filing system, a filing cabinet with drawers and folders. Within a drawer, each item had a folder, and the folders were arranged alphabetically. Occasionally a folder would be added, or one removed. Mentally, I could simply go through the alphabet and see each folder under the letters. I could stop at a folder, pull it out, open it up and go over the contents, make some changes, put it back in the drawer, and go on.

Much like The Jukebox for music, it was a way to retain information and a sort of plan of action once I was free.

Over time the list grew, and, by the time of my release, the drawer contained seventy-seven folders.

A—Art, Aviation, Autos

B— Boating, Books, Bowling, Business, Buying

C—Camping, Career, Cards, Ceremony, Civics, Clothes, Cooking, Correspondence

D—Dancing, Dining, Drinking, Diary

E— Education, Entertainment

F— Family, Friends, Finance, Fishing

G—Geography, Golf, Guns, Guitar

H—Handball, Health, History, Hobbies, Homes

I— Information, Investment, Insurance

K—Kommunication

L— Languages, Leadership

M—Math, Memory, Music

N—News

O—Organizations, Opportunity

P— Patriotism, Periodicals, Photography, Philosophy, Politics, Professional, Psychology

Q—Quotations

R—Religion, Retirement, Retreat, Romance

S— Savior, Sailing, Skiing, Scuba, Smoking,
   Speech, Stereo
T—Tapes, Tennis, Time, Travel, Typing
U—Update
V—V.A., Vacations
W—Writing, Wife
X—Xercise

Truck to the Dogpatch

In November 1968, President Johnson halted Operation Rolling Thunder, the major bombing campaign against North Vietnam, and announced at about the same time that he would not run for re-election. Since the peace talks were going on in Paris, most of us thought he had reached an agreement for our release. This was not the case, however, and when we realized this we felt abandoned, since the war against the North essentially was over. This gave the North Vietnamese more than four years to rebuild, re-arm and step up their supply of weapons and materials to the Viet Cong via the Ho Chi Minh Trail, and send regular North Vietnamese Army troops into the South.

In the spring of 1972, North Vietnam launched the Easter Campaign, an outright invasion of South Vietnam, with thousands of troops, tanks, and artillery. In response, in April President Nixon launched Operation Linebacker, renewing the bombing of North Vietnam by B-52s.

Following the Son Tay Raid, almost all POWs were held in the Hanoi Hilton, and it is my belief that the North Vietnamese feared that if the prison were bombed by B-52s they could lose about the only bargaining chips they had—that is, *us*, the American prisoners of war.

On May 13, 1972, some 220 of us, about half the total number of POWs, were loaded onto trucks for the 109-mile trip to a remote prison in Cao Bang Province, close to the Chinese border. The trip took three miserable days. We were handcuffed in pairs and crammed, about twenty to a truck, along with all the supplies and equipment needed to set up the prison. Hubie Buchanan and I were cuffed together, and we were right beside a fifty-five-gallon drum of gasoline. The road was in terrible shape, causing the truck to lurch and bounce, which in turn caused the gasoline to seep out even though the drum appeared to be sealed. The fumes were overpowering, and by the end of the trip we were all nauseated, and one or two guys had vomited, making things even worse.

What was scary was the fact that there were two guards sitting at the back of the truck smoking. In addition to the misery of the handcuffs, the gasoline, the cramped position, no water or food, sickness and only one pit stop each day, my real fear was that we were going to die in an inferno. Sitting on our bedrolls with all our stuff rolled up in the sleeping mat, I could get to my hidden "tool kit" and retrieve my razor blade. With it, I cut cross-shaped slits in the canvas cover of the truck. At night, when the guards were not looking, I could open these for a little ventilation and a look outside. I was afraid the Vietnamese would discover the slits and trace them back to me, but they never did.

Somehow the gasoline did not ignite, and we did get a little water and some salted fish, but we were ready to riot by the end of the trip, and we made that clear to the guards.

This was certainly the worst trip of my life, and when we got to The Dogpatch I was grateful to be back in a cell with a wooden bed board. The cellblocks were scattered haphazardly around the hilly prison compound. I was originally in a group of twenty-one, with John Stavast as the SRO (his code name was Buckeye). In October I moved to another cellblock and the SRO

The remote prison in the mountainous area near the Chinese border that the POWs called The Dogpatch. The author was held in the two cellblocks marked with bold borders. *Sketch done by author*

was Bob Purcell (code name: Aladdin). There were seventeen of us in this group.

The Green Sweater

Summer and fall in the mountainous area close to China were cooler and drier than in Hanoi, but as winter approached in 1972, it became much colder and we were given a third, thin cotton blanket. I received several packages from Marty while I was at The Dogpatch. Some guys got long underwear in packages as well as socks and T-shirts, but nothing like that came for me.

One day in late November or early December, the turnkey opened the door to our courtyard and signaled me to come outside. This was usually a sign that something bad was about to happen, but this time he handed me a green sweater, without a word. I knew instantly that this was the sweater Marty had been knitting for me and had described in detail in our correspondence before I was shot down. I was overjoyed! I now had something warm to wear, and it was handmade by Marty.

It was not until I came home that I learned more of the story behind the sweater. After Marty was told that I had been killed, she gave the unfinished sweater to a friend whose husband was in the Air Force. When Marty learned in 1967 that I might not have died and was probably a POW, the friend returned the sweater, which she had finished.

Since POWs are supposed to receive letters and packages through the International Red Cross, Marty mailed the sweater to me in the first package she sent in

1967. So, it was incredible that the North Vietnamese had kept the sweater in a storage bin somewhere with my name on it for all that time and then brought it all the way up to The Dogpatch some five years later to give to me. It certainly made me wonder what else they had in that bin.

When I wore the sweater with the dickey I had made from the pair of red socks I had received in a previous package, I was probably the most sartorially splendid POW in Hanoi. I brought the sweater and dickey home with me, and for many years I wore them on Christmas Day.

The green sweater that the author's wife, Marty, started knitting for him while he was still on the cruise. Hearing later that he'd been killed, she gave it to another wife to finish, but got it back when she heard he was alive—and sent it. Prison officials didn't pass it along for four years.

Ghost Story

There was no electricity at The Dogpatch, so at night we were mostly in the dark. The Vietnamese did give us these very small kerosene lamps, the kind with a wick that could be adjusted with a wheel to make it brighter or dimmer. The little glass container held less than a half cup of kerosene, which was only replenished once a week. When we went to bed, the lamp was turned down so there was just a blue glow to show where it was. If you got up to use the bucket, you could turn it up enough to see, but then turn it back down. That way we could make it last for the entire seven days.

In the evenings we told movies and stories, and when my turn came I decided to tell a ghost story. It was a creepy one, and the tension built and built to a very dramatic and sudden conclusion.

Marty had sent a pair of bright red boxer shorts in a package, and I was wearing them that night. The cotton fabric was thin, so they were quite comfortable compared to the clothes the Vietnamese had provided.

I was sitting on the end of one of the wooden bed-boards with my back against the wall. The lamp was turned down very low, adding to the ghostly atmosphere, and I was speaking in a low and eerie-sounding voice. I came to the conclusion of my story and was about to burst out with the dramatic ending when I felt something bite me on my butt. I let out a yell that everyone thought was part of the story but realized it wasn't when I jumped up with a foot-long centipede attached to my shorts. Several guys took their rubber sandals and began hammering this gigantic insect, cutting it into several pieces. We really panicked when each of these pieces began scurrying off in different directions. More hammering with the sandals finally ended the drama, with squashed bug all over the floor. We could see that the piece with the head had huge, sharp pincers that had latched onto me, but did not break the skin. Thank goodness, because I later learned that such East Asian centipedes—*Scolopendra subspinipes*—are quite venomous and can be deadly.

This area had many other venomous creatures, including snakes and a very deadly lizard of which the Vietnamese were terrified. All the guards in the camp wore high boots, carried sticks, and were on high alert when they heard the lizard's distinctive call—a powerful shriek that seemed to come from everywhere in the trees.

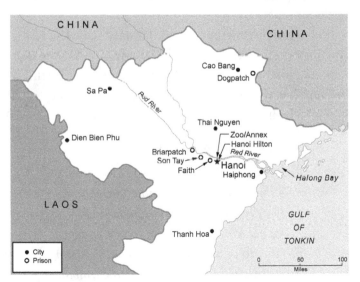

North Vietnam in 1965, showing major cities and POW prisons—including the Hanoi Hilton, Briarpatch, Son Tay, Camp Faith, The Zoo, The Zoo Annex, and Dogpatch. *Created by Chris Robinson*

After this incident, we plugged up the drain holes in our cells, since we were sure this was how the centipede got in.

Hanoi Journal

Most of us in The Dogpatch believed we would not go back to Hanoi until the United States had stopped the bombing, and that the bombing would not stop until the Vietnamese had agreed to sign the peace treaty. When it became clear that peace was really at hand, I began making notes on scraps of paper with my pencil stubs. The notes eventually grew into my Hanoi Journal, a diary I kept of events leading up to our release from North Vietnam on February 12, 1973 and the arrival of our "Freedom Bird" at Clark Air Force Base in the Philippines.

The bombing stopped on January 16, 1973, my thirty-second birthday. As I thought about the significance of the event and how wonderful a birthday present it was, I also began to think about what it was going to be like to step back into freedom.

METAMORPHOSIS

Trembling and silent before the threshold,
We stand on the eve of our resurrection.
Hardly daring to believe that at last
The valve may crack and we may seep
Into the tip of an infinitely expanding horn,
To be belched into that crowded carnival,
An old song.

She stands before me, silent, across the wide river:
Her smile seen dimly through the damp fog.
Watching through my peephole, I can only
Whisper her name—Freedom . . .
And I, within my hardened shell,
Await Rebirth.

(JANUARY 1973)

At first the journal notes were written on various pieces of paper, depending on what was available. The Vietnamese were required to provide each POW with a copy of the January 27, 1973 Paris Peace Accords, so the backs of these pages became my journal once we got back to Hanoi. I had stolen some of the Vietnamese ink that came in little packets of powder to be mixed with water, and I made a pen from bamboo.

In the diary notes, I used many abbreviations. Initials stood for individuals, especially in the notes prior to our release. Some initials refer to code names for buildings in the compound, others are for guards and interrogators, and still others are simply shorthand for longer words.

The following is that journal, edited for brevity and clarity:

18 JAN. 1973 DOGPATCH

We are wakened in the middle of the night by the sound of trucks arriving in camp. The arrival of trucks has only confirmed the many signs of a coming move over the past few days.

19 Jan. Fri.

Bob Purcell, our SRO, is up at dawn and will not let anyone else sleep he is so excited. We prepare a mobility plan and begin to arrange our gear for the trip. After supper, we pack and wait. Travel chow of sticky rice and meat arrives.

20 Jan. Sat.

After midnight, Vietnamese come and say we will move tonight. We settled in the truck about 2:30 a.m. and got on the road about 4:00. The roads are much better than they were on the trip up to Dogpatch, but we are very crowded as there are 20 of us in the truck. I am handcuffed to Marty Neuens. The truck is covered by a tarp, and I again make "windows" with my razor blade. As dawn breaks, we are following the course of a large river. The scenery is beautiful, but it is sharply contrasted by the mud-hut villages. Thousands of trucks are parked along the road, along with road repair equipment. This time we have water in the truck and can smoke. The truck stopped twice for chow and head-calls, and we got out of cuffs each time. I even got to brush my teeth and wash my face. The last chow stop is about 10 K north of Thai Nguyen, and just after that we begin to see the first bomb damage. I discovered a deck of American playing cards in one of the guards' packs. Since it was obviously pilfered from one of our packages from home, I stole it back. Coming into Hanoi, we cross two long pontoon bridges across the Red River, and we can see the downed bridges up the river. What a beautiful sight! On the second bridge, we stop in the middle as traffic is held up. Two girls are bailing out barges. One of the guards we call Johnny Longrifle has been flirting with everything female along the way and he goes into high gear now. We are the first truck to arrive at the Hanoi Hilton at about 11:00 pm. [The] Elf and many other Vietnamese are there at the gate to "welcome" us. Room 6 of Camp Unity is already occupied by Americans, and we freely talk as we move into Room 4. It is the same room we were in before, but now it has tables, stools, and bed boards. The bamboo screens are gone from the windows and courtyards. Another truckload follows us into the room for a total of 40 in Room 4. The Vietnamese have bread waiting for us and tell us we can bathe. We stole 10 kilos of cereal bars ("Gorilla Food") from our truck and shared that with everyone in the room and then destroyed the evidence.

21 JAN. SUN.

Rooms 1, 2, and 3 have Fall '66 to Summer '67 shoot-downs, while Rooms 4, 6, and 7 have the "old heads." There are now 234 prisoners in Unity, with the 141 from Dogpatch. The new guys shot down during the recent bombing moved out the night we moved in, but there is lots of secondhand news from these new shootdowns. We are astounded at the news of the B-52 raids, smart bombs, changes in morality, and all the new styles. All the fences are down in camp, and a basketball/volleyball court and new ping-pong rooms are up. POWs work in the kitchen, but do KP only, like at [The] Dogpatch.

22 JAN. MON.

We are out in the big courtyard in the morning with Rms. 6 and 7 and Rms. 1, 2, and 3 are out together in the afternoon. I saw many old friends for the first time, face-to-face, and Fred Cherry and I were together for the first time in 5½ years! Beautiful weather, warm.

Vietnamese say that the peace agreements have not
been signed yet.

23 JAN. TUES.
Vietnamese say that Freddie Frederick is in the hospital.

24 JAN. WED.
I played volleyball and ping-pong today for the first
time.

25 JAN. THURS.
The Vietnamese camp commander talks to the whole
camp, "If Nixon thinks carefully, there may be peace,
etc." We are allowed to mix afterward, and I think the
speech was only an excuse to let us talk to each other,
which is the same old "step-by-step" Vietnamese
program.

26 JAN. FRI.
A slow day. Vietnamese attitude has been surprisingly
consistent in view of recent events. Turnkeys are their
same old arrogant, disagreeable selves. I am surprised,
but pleasantly so. I want to leave NVN with the same
bitter taste in my mouth that I have had all these years.
Quincy Collins started work on my song for "Marty."

27 JAN. SAT.
John Borling gives the first of the new movies from
the new shootdowns, "Play Misty for Me." Later in
the evening, the lights on the antenna tower come on
(for the first time in many months) and we hear bands
playing, crowds cheering, etc. Most of us think that
it's all over now.

28 JAN. SUN.
This morning we witnessed a wonderful sight, the
Vietnamese flag flying from the tower upside down!

They change it, but not before all in camp have seen it. They won't say if agreements have been signed or not, but we think they have.

29 Jan. Mon.

The Vietnamese camp commander reads the announcement that the agreements have been signed to half of camp at a time. One of our interrogators, Spot, interprets for him. We hear the same thing on the radio many times. Vietnamese move furniture (beds, tables, stools, bookcases, etc.) into Room 5 storage. We think this furniture was used by the wounded POWs. We get American magazines and some ping-pong balls. Smitty Harris sees what he thinks is an American C-130 coming in. A jeep brings bundles into Room 5. We think they are our "go-home" clothes because we see the belts.

30 Jan. Tues.

We are each given a copy of the peace agreement that was signed by the four parties on Jan. 27 in Paris. A guard says that the bundles in Room 5 are our clothes. We use the back of the agreements as writing paper. Quincy finishes his four-part arrangement of "Marty."

31 Jan. Wed.

Today I have [spent] 2,363 days in Vietnam. Packages arrive in camp. We wash the leaves for the Banh Chung (sticky rice cake prepared for the Tet Lunar New Year).

1 Feb. Thurs.

We get packages in the afternoon. They are handled in the same manner as always. Vietnamese steal the same things from them and say, "the packages are still bad." Early in the morning, I wrote "Metamorphosis."

2 FEB. FRI.

Play basketball and, of course, get a blister. I have KP in the afternoon and cut onions for Tet meal. We got Banh Chung and, this year for the first time, I gave it all away. Camp commander has a quiz with John Flynn, Robbie Risner, and all the room SROs. This is a first and a long-awaited event. The Vietnamese promise there will be no propaganda, cameras, or reporters in the prison camp. They are concerned that we will make a bad scene (demonstration) when we leave camp, but we promise not to if they keep their promise. Some in the room play poker all night. There is a fireworks display for Tet at midnight.

3 FEB. SAT.

The moon is new; the first day of Tet. We have a "big meal," but it is the same as always and the bread is stale. We get the pictures that came in the packages, not in plastic this time.

4 FEB. SUN.

We are measured for shoes. It's beginning to finally dawn on me that we indeed may be going home soon, but I am still afraid to let my guard down too much. We see some C-130s. Our light is out and the electrical system in general in camp is in bad shape. What a day!

5 FEB. MON.

Some got old and new letters, but I did not. More clothes are stored in Room 5. I washed the green sweater. The lights are very dim, so I go to bed early.

6 FEB. TUES.

Old letters come in by the handful. I got 13 that I had never seen before, and one was dated 1967. More clothes and shoes arrive. Some of us go into Room 5 as the Vietnamese are working with the clothes and they let us try on shoes. We see lots of Dien Bien cigarettes, soap, toothpaste, and towels. Risner has another quiz. Two of the interrogators, Mazola and Spot, say we will leave in five days. That puts it right on schedule according to the agreements. Play some volleyball. We turn in a list of men, "small, medium and large," for clothes. Vietnamese are now working more and more through our senior officers. At night, we read articles from *Saturday Review* on the war. Again, the lights are dim. Seven men from Blue and Rawhide leave camp at night. This is a further reshuffle of groups by shootdown date. It appears that the original groups are getting smaller for some unknown reason. I work on the diary.

7 Feb. Wed.

Vietnamese say more men will move tonight. We get soap and toothpaste. Finish packing. Ran in the afternoon. I promise to make calls for Glen Nix and Irv Williams when I get home as they will be in a later group. More men move, so we are now down to 32. More old mail. Practice departure formation for the second time.

8 Feb. Thurs.

Raining and turning colder. We hear that Kissinger is to arrive in Hanoi on the 10th and stay until the 13th. Many people think and hope that he will meet us at the release. A song and dance group start[s] moving gear into camp. Flynn and Risner already told the Vietnamese we will not attend a live performance in camp. Robbie tells them that he hopes the show brought its own audience. They say it is for guards, but we can go if we want. Robbie has a stand-up quiz with camp commander and Soft Soap Fairy (interrogator). Many Vietnamese are in camp, and they try to talk us into going to the show. Robbie and Larry Guarino have a quiz with a high-powered Vietnamese who says a U.S. admiral will arrive Wednesday on a C-130, then go to Haiphong for de-mining operations. There are fifty ships de-mining now. The first group will be released during Kissinger's visit. Vietnamese try hard again to get us to go to the show. The show begins after dark on the volleyball court. Robbie has a quiz during the show. We do not watch the show. Vietnamese take our stools for the show, and, at intermission, Elf begs our room to go.

9 FEB. FRI.

The whole camp is out together for the first time. Robbie speaks to the entire group, and then he has another quiz. Vietnamese threaten to ruin his life and career if we slander The Democratic Republic of Vietnam (DRV). This contrasts with last night's quiz where they almost apologized for our bad treatment. Stockdale and Denton both have blackmail quizzes with Cat, who is speaking for Maj. Bai. Kay Russell and the group sing Quincy Collins' arrangement of "Marty."

10 FEB. SAT.

Up at the crack of dawn. Hard to get to sleep last night. (I wonder why!) I run, do handstands, take a bath, and serve milk. Soft Soap Fairy says we will not go tomorrow, but soon. Bill Robinson has a quiz and the Vietnamese say no U.S. troops have left SVN yet and we will go when they do. Kissinger is here to talk about reconstruction. Bill Robinson is given stamps with his picture on them. Hey, Rube!! (the warning that there are cameras) is yelled because two white reporters (French and German?) with cameras, and many Vietnamese reporters come into the camp. Everyone runs back into the cells. They talk to Risner and Stockdale through the cell door and take some pictures. No one else will talk to them. Many think we will leave tonight; who knows? I talk with friends about what we will do first day home. Overhear two guys talk about getting revenge on Vietnamese. Not what I want at all.

11 FEB. SUN.

Shumaker has been a POW for eight years today, and there are eight turkeys in camp for a big meal tonight. Wedding rings are returned to guys in cells [Nos.] 4, 6, and 7. Hatcher got $17 back. Robbie has a quiz with a DRV government representative who says we will get clothes tonight and shave. Early in the morning, we will leave altogether for the airport (Phuc Yen). We will get bags and toilet articles in the morning. I take the last bath and shave after I get my go-home clothes. I modify the belt, clip my nails. Tomorrow, the sweet taste of freedom.

12 FEB. MON.

We are up at 5 AM to be ready to leave at 6:00. Last night Brian Wood[s] moved into Cell 7. His mom is very ill and both governments agree to his early release. We move from [Camp] Unity to the Heartbreak court-yard at about 6:00 AM. We are given overnight bags with towels, soap, toothpaste, toothbrush, 2 packs of Dien Bien cigarettes, and matches. Then we sit on benches and wait for about an hour. Get word that Wilber and Miller are in the New Guy Village group, suited up and ready to go. Ray Vohden has them in tow. We finally march through the main gate at about 7:20. Before I get on the bus, I turn back to Hoa Lo Prison, that place of misery and hatred, and I say, "I forgive you." All the hatred that I have nurtured for the North Vietnamese for over seven years disappears, and I walk away from two prisons. People begin to form at the square and the cops try to break it up. One man has a movie camera, but the guards take it away from him. I sit in the front of the bus with Ralph Gaither. We leave at 7:35. There is a motorcycle with a sidecar, two ambulances, a jeep, and then the buses. There are 20 of us on the 4th bus. The sick and injured are on the first bus. We drive through the French section of town with wide streets, old French homes, and government buildings. We see a few cameras after we have gone a block or two. It is overcast and windy. We cross a pontoon bridge at 7:50 (5 min.). There is a small check station at the end of this bridge and two photographers are there with movie cameras. We think the reporters are Japanese. See the airport at 8:05 as we are driving along the dike. There are many people on bikes. Arrive at the waiting station (somewhere on airport grounds) at 8:30. The building has several rooms, and we are in one that is like an old bus station with benches. The sick and injured are in a separate room. There is a Red Cross tent just outside; we think for the litter cases. See a MiG 17 crank up. Vietnamese pass out tea and pig fat sandwiches. I wouldn't have eaten it but I was starving! Smoke pipe, brush teeth (about 10:00), and start to write. Vietnamese pass out beer. Wash hands and final head call (there is a separate building with toilet facilities). Back on the bus at about 11:52. The bus in front of us is B1S-004. We see a C-141 landing right in front of us. Very short distance to the runway, past the terminal, which is in shambles from bomb damage. Fox [a senior officer in prison administration] is in the sidecar, and he has a guard with a field phone. We park on a ramp area; the 141 is about 100 yards away with the tailgate down. The litter cases go aboard first and then the CI's (sick and injured). Our bus is next as I am writing (12:15). Funny feeling in my stomach. Hundreds of people, many with cameras, around the C-141. At 12:20, another 141 makes an approach and goes around. Aircraft #50243 lands at 12:24 right beside us. To the right of us, across the runway are some old aircraft and a small radar site. At 12:29, the first 141 (60177, 3rd MAW) taxies and starts to roll at 12:35. Liftoff right beside us. Our bus moves forward, left turn, off the bus. We approached the turnover area and Rabbit reads our names, one by one. My name is read, and I cross the line to salute Col. Lynn. Freedom! And now it's real. Dave Wheat and I walk to the 141 with Bill Waters (Air Force enlisted).

Dave Wheat and author (*left*) at the loading ramp of the C-141 "Freedom Bird." *USAF*

Onboard at 12:45. Turn up at 12:50. Start to roll at 1:00. Brief by Flight Surgeon and Nurse, Pat O'Reilly. The [captain announces] that the 3rd 141 is on the ground at Gia Lam. The first cigarette, which I really didn't want, was a long Marlboro. It was strong. Can of "Redwood Empire" apple juice. Benson & Hedges and a cup of coffee. I am sitting with Dave Wheat and Robbie Risner.

Dave Wheat and author (*left*) on board the C-141. *USAF*

Robbie moves to talk to the public affairs officer. Lights come on for movies and pix, then we settle back for a three-hour trip to Clark AFB. I read [an article in] the Philippine Flyer about our homecoming. It is hard to hold back the tears. Now that it's here it's almost anti-climactic. Talk to Jim Parrie, who was in the same preflight class as Alcorn. Start letdown at 4:25 local time. It is warm at Clark, so we will get off in shirtsleeves. Our reception at Clark is indescribable and wonderful. Thousands of people, all waving signs, banners, flags, yelling, "We love you, Welcome Home." We get off one by one, and after salutes and handshakes with CINCPAC [Commander in Chief, U.S. Forces, Pacific] and others, Robbie speaks for us, eloquently as usual, and we get into special [buses] and drive to the hospital. What a drive, with people lining the roads, waving, saluting, pouring out their hearts for us, the most exhilarating and happiest ride of my life. And now we begin our lives again . . . at long last.

One Step Closer to Home
CLARK AIR FORCE BASE
THE PHILIPPINES—12–16 FEB.

The halls of the hospital at Clark Air Force Base in the Philippines were covered with hundreds, if not thousands, of signs, banners, and cards, all welcoming us home, along with many Valentine's Day cards. One of these cards was signed by Gary, a sixth-grade student, and the sentiment he expressed for us was so powerful and moving, I incorporated some of his words into a poem of thanks that I wrote on the flight from the Philippines to San Francisco. It was almost too much to take in, but it didn't take long until I felt I had really shed captivity.

I was in a room with Brad Smith, and Fred Cherry was right down the hall. I found out later that a couple of guys had gotten Fred drunk, and he had passed out. They laid him out like a corpse with a flower in his folded arms and sounded the alarm for the nurse. This caused quite a stir, but it was just fighter pilots being fighter pilots.

I was determined to scrub away every molecule of Vietnam before I got back to Marty and Dabney, so I took eight hot, soapy showers in the first two days. What a luxury that was!

We were fitted for uniforms to wear for the flight home, and some of us went to the PX (Post Exchange) to buy civilian clothes, gifts, and other things. I got the latest Nikon camera, an emerald ring for Marty, and a portable radio for Dabney. The civilian clothes looked bizarre, ugly, and unfamiliar to me, but I tried some on anyway. Everything was double-knit, bell-bottomed, and garish. While I was standing at the full-length mirror trying to decide if I could actually wear an outfit like that, I failed to notice the TV camera crew filming me from behind.

Many guys made phone calls home that first day and the next, but I was told that I had to see the chaplain first. I was sure my grandparents had died, but I did not know for sure about my mother. He confirmed that she had died in 1968. The fact that the chaplain took his time setting up the meeting to inform me was the only sour spot in our stay at Clark. After that, Marty and I spent many hours on the phone. She asked if I intended to fly again and I said no. That was certainly the answer she wanted to hear, and I kept my word.

I told her about trying on the clothes, and she said she had seen it on TV. She only saw me from the back, but she was sure it was me. The camera had started at my feet with the big brass buckles on the shoes. Then it moved up to the plaid bell-bottom double-knit pants, with a white belt. The shirt also was double-knit with garish yellow plaid and a big collar. I was glad they had not shown my face.

I was soon to learn that styles were not the only things that had radically changed since 1965, and adapting to them was going to take some time.

We stayed at Clark AFB in the Philippines for four days for medical exams and treatment, debriefing, uni-form fittings, and lots of time on the phone with family.

Another Step Closer

When we left Clark Air Force Base for the long flight to Travis Air Force Base in the San Francisco Bay Area, it was again on board a C-141, and I was grateful that ours was fitted with stretchers in addition to the seats so I could get some sleep.

I felt such profound gratitude for our release after so many years. I tried to think of a way to say thank you to all Americans who had prayed for us, had worn the POW/MIA bracelets, had written letters to our cap-tors asking for better treatment, and had supported us and our families in so many ways. The poem of thanks I wrote over the Pacific Ocean as I got closer and closer to home was printed in many newspapers that carried stories about our release and welcome home.

FREEDOM

A newborn, reborn child of joy,
I step from my cell into your arms,
Your lives, your love,
Your soontobemine world,

Our country . . .
Freedom . . . too sweet for paltry words . . .
But now I try . . . to you we must express . . .
Can I, for all, say thank you . . . ?
Again my paltry words will fail.
One, two, three, 2, hundred . . . million . . .
One to infinity for each . . . . Thank you.

Our suffering . . . feel no pity . . .
Please, no pity . . . We stand tall
For you . . . with you.
My hand quivers, joydrops wet my face,
The lump is always there . . .
The apple of joy and love . . .
For you . . . and freedom.

Just now I read . . . to me . . . to us:
"Dear Sir,
I sure am glad
Your all done . . .
I said a prayer every night . . .
And it finally came true.
Welcome home sir.
I would have
Gave my life
To get you guys out of there
But I don't think my parents
Would like it.
I think you'll like being home
With your family.
I'm a six grader.
Gary"

Many died in Vietnam . . . gave their lives . . .
Love them . . . honor them . . .
Please honor them . . .
They won't be coming home.
We are here because of you . . .
My paltry words have failed . . .
But . . . I must try
To say
Thank you.

(FEBRUARY 16, 1973—C-141)
PORTER HALYBURTON

We stopped to refuel in Hawaii in the middle of the night and were welcomed by local military and civilian officials. Although we were on U.S. soil for the first time and overjoyed to be there, it did not feel quite like home just yet. When we landed in San Francisco, we were also welcomed by a large crowd of well wishers and the local military brass. After refreshments and lots of handshakes, we boarded smaller aircraft for flights to military bases across the country that were located closest to our homes. The naval hospital at Jacksonville, Florida, was the closest one to Atlanta, where Marty and Dabney were living. Along the way, we landed at several bases where I could watch from the plane as guys were greeted on the tarmac by their families and hordes of reporters and cameramen.

The pilot of the plane was able to establish radio contact with Marty, who was waiting in the control tower at Naval Air Station Jacksonville, so I was able to talk to her before we arrived. We both agreed that we wanted our reunion to be private rather than a public spectacle such as I had witnessed along the way. At this point, Ralph Gaither and I were the only ones left on the plane.

As the plane approached, Marty was monitoring everything from the control tower and watching the crowds gathering for our arrival. As we landed, she was taken to the hospital to wait for me in the room that had been specially prepared for us, with furniture, flowers, and pictures of Dabney. There was also a tape recorder set up to capture our reunion. Dabney, now almost eight years old, was staying with some friends in their home nearby.

Home at Last

As I was escorted from the plane to the hospital, my heart was pounding with anticipation and excitement. I was coming home, because home for me was anywhere Marty was. As I stepped into the room and the door was shut quietly behind me, the sight of her opened the floodgate of joyful tears, and she leaped into my arms—arms that had been waiting so long to feel her touch once again. We were both so glad that we had this joyous moment together in private.

I never spent a night in this room, which was four rooms put together, because I did not have health problems aside from intestinal worms. The base had arranged for a special cottage for us on the grounds of the hospital, so we stayed there for a month except for a few days at a beach house some friends lent us.

The next morning I was so anxious to see Dabney that we drove over to the house where she was staying and picked her up. Marty was driving, since my driver's license had somehow expired. As soon as we got in the car, Dabney asked, "Daddy, can I sit in your lap?" I had been afraid that she might find me somewhat of a stranger at first, but that was not the case at all. We were friends from that moment on.

The three of us spent nearly three magical weeks together in Jacksonville before returning to Atlanta. The Navy had prepared a great deal of information to help us ex-POWs get caught up with things that had happened while we were gone, and there were so many books to read that I was overwhelmed, but also so very grateful. I found out that the next group of returnees would be arriving in a few days and that Irv Williams would be among them, so I delayed our return to Atlanta to be there to welcome him and the others home, and for him to meet Marty and Dabney. Another joyous reunion.

Marty, Dabney, and Porter arrive in Atlanta. *AP Wire, 1973*

Epilogue

Looking Back

IN THE AFTERMATH OF LONG CAPTIVITY, SUFFERING, AND difficult times, I thought a lot about how we were able to survive—and not only to survive, but to "Survive with Honor" and to "Return with Honor," as had become our creed. I tried so hard always to stay active—mentally, physically, and spiritually—and I think this was a very important aspect of my survival. Along with the other POWs, I also made it my daily mission to deny the Vietnamese the control over our lives that they tried to establish through propaganda, indoctrination, degradation, intimidation, fear, deprivation, threats, isolation, boredom, pain, and lies. When all of those tactics generally failed, the Vietnamese resorted to extreme violence and torture. Most of us found ways to continue to resist and defy them by adopting a "Second Line of Resistance."

Our "First Line of Resistance" was to say no and refuse to do or say anything that might be harmful to our country, our families, or our fellow POWs. However, we learned the painful reality that our captors had all the time in the world to inflict a level of pain and terror that we had not imagined, and that there would be a limit to our endurance. When that limit was reached and you had to do or say something, the "Second Line" reminded you that there was usually something that you could do in order to render their tactics useless in turning public opinion against the war, especially in America. Ultimately, torture and mistreatment did not serve them well.

One advantage we had—and a weapon we could use—was our captors' poor understanding of American culture, humor, sign language, and the very fabric of our society. All the interrogators spoke English and some, like The Rabbit, spoke it well, but none of them spoke American. None of them had even been to the United States. We used this ignorance against them in our "Second Line of Resistance."

I would have loved to have been there when some Russian or Chinese intelligence analyst reviewed all the photos the guards had taken of us and explained to the Vietnamese what a raised middle finger meant!

There were no constraints to their treatment of us. They denied that any international laws or organizations had jurisdiction—neither the Geneva Conventions nor the International Red Cross. However, the weapons and defenses that we had were quite powerful.

Certainly, our homogeneity was a positive factor. We were almost exclusively aviators of some kind, most of us had college educations, all were volunteers, most of us were very patriotic, and we had great reason to support our government, our democratic way of life, and the sources of prosperity and freedom.

We were fortunate that we had capable leaders at every level of command—men who led by example, not just by the orders they issued or the advice they gave. For us, that was normal. Leaders of any rank or authority must have communication with those they lead, and without it leadership and command do not mean much. Left on our own without communication, we would have been much more susceptible to the North Vietnamese efforts to control and use us as part of their war effort. That's why our captors tried so hard to isolate us from our leaders and from one another. They brutalized and isolated our senior leadership, denied that we had ranks at all, and treated us as criminals. Without men like Robbie Risner, Jim Stockdale, Jerry Denton, Bob Purcell and others, we could have been lost. Had our leaders been weaker men without the courage, wisdom, and determination that was necessary, I shudder to think how much more difficult it would have been. At the working level, the senior ranking officer was the one who commanded a group with which he had regular communication— usually a cellblock—but he ultimately reported to an even more senior officer with whom he might be in touch more sporadically.

Our covert networks of communication were our salvation. No matter how difficult they were or how many times they were disrupted, they always survived. If we became professional at anything, it was communication, and its use spanned the spectrum of life and activity. We also vowed to never let a brother fall outside the net; never let one fall through the crack; never say our situation was just too hard.

Our collective wealth of knowledge, experience, wisdom, and creativity, bolstered by so many men with great courage, determination, and spirituality, helped us over time to build a culture and a society that had many of the characteristics of normal society, for we had become a family—a family held together and supported through a difficult communications network.

My own adaptation to life in prison occurred in three phases, and the edges between them were not distinct. They merged from one to the next without my realizing it had happened until I looked back and saw how my attitude and perspective had changed over my seven-plus years in captivity.

In the beginning, when most of us were quite sanguine and naive about how long the war would last and much less optimistic about how long we could survive, my thoughts were primarily about the past, and I tried to recall every detail of my life. I wanted to recapture the joy and happiness of the experiences that I had had and the people I had known. Living in my past was a way to escape from the grim reality of the present. Along with all the good memories came the realization that I had wasted a great deal of time and had missed opportunities because of my laziness and my preoccupation with having fun. Worst of all, I had to admit how badly I had treated some people—especially my mother and grandparents, who had done so much for me—and how little I had done for them, hurting and disappointing them in many ways.

From the anguish that I felt about the faults and errors of my youth came a determination that my future life (if I were to have a future life) would be different, and that I would try to make amends, to be the best husband I could be to Marty, the best father I could be to Dabney, and to live my life in a positive and productive way. My thoughts turned from the past to the future and how to make all this a reality. In the end, I had my list of seventy-seven categories of interests, activities, and goals.

Since the past had been my escape from the painful and uncertain present, living in the future also became the way to escape it. This second phase of my adaptation was certainly more positive, more productive, and more hopeful because I realized that I had survived for a longer time than I had thought I could and had endured much more than I had thought was possible. Living in this imaginary future was much more pleasant than living in a very real and difficult present. I still thought that any meaningful life for me would begin when I was free. Many conversations would begin with "When I get out of here, . . ."

The transition from this phase to the final one probably began when I moved in with that wonderful bunch of guys, The Onagers. The nine of us had never been in this kind of group situation, and I think it had the same effect on all of us. Together we had the resources to deal with the present, to think about and plan for the activities for each day, to consider how we could improve our lives by teaching each other what we knew, and to grow to love and respect each other in our diversity.

Although I moved away from The Onagers to other groups, I never lost that sense of community and the feeling that "We are all in this together, so let's make the most of it while we are here." Every person was a brother, a resource, a part of the family.

In the beginning, I did not see how I could endure two months of captivity. The longer I was there, my projected release date moved further out in relation to how long I thought I could endure—from two years at first, then to three, and later to four. All this time I still thought that my freedom held the key to my happiness, and I grasped at every straw of hope that release might be imminent. My spirits would rise each time the food got better or when there was a medical exam, a foreign delegation was touring the prison, there was some good news from a new POW, or some other reason to hope the end of captivity was near. When nothing happened, my spirits would plummet into depression. That resulted in a sort of sine wave of elation and depression, and the roller coaster of emotions was difficult. My remedy for this was to adopt what I called long-term, nonspecific optimism, which was a way of saying: "I believe we will get out of here sometime, but there is nothing I can do to make it happen, and worrying about when will not make it happen any sooner." From that point on, I felt that I could survive and lead a meaningful life for at least ten more years, and I was prepared to spend the rest of my life in prison if necessary and still feel that my life was not a waste. Such is the power of human adaptation and the urge to find meaning in one's life.

That became clear to me after reading *Man's Search for Meaning*, by Viktor Frankl, after I came home. Frankl had survived Auschwitz, the Nazi concentration camp, but had witnessed misery and death beyond anything we had known in Vietnam, and as a psychoanalyst and keen observer of human behavior, Frankl felt that a person could find meaning in life even in the worst of circumstances. Man's basic urge is to discover the meaning in one's life, and one of the most powerful ways of doing that was through suffering, Frankl wrote. He stressed that it is not so important what happens to you, or what you have or do not have, but it *is* important how you react to your circumstances, what choices you make, and the attitude you have about life.

That is what happened to me in the prisons of North Vietnam, but it took Frankl to explain how it had happened and what it meant.

Lessons Learned the Hard Way

After I left the naval hospital in Jacksonville, Florida, and we went to Atlanta, where Marty and Dabney had been living since shortly after my shootdown, when they thought I had been killed, a reporter asked if I could sum up my experience in a few words. I thought for a few minutes, then said, "I would not do it again for a million dollars, but I would not take a million dollars for having done it." I had learned so much of importance to my life that I might not have learned otherwise, and I was extremely grateful for that, and for the friends I now had—a true band of brothers.

When I thought about all of this and tried to make sense of it, I realized that our lives were determined more by the choices that we made rather than by the circumstances of our captivity. I also learned that this was true for human life in any circumstance. Our free will and the freedom to choose our reaction to any condition or event was something that could not be taken away from us except by despair, insanity, or death. I saw how critical this was in my decision to always choose the Worst Place, and how different my entire life would be had I chosen the Better Place.

So, I learned the first great lesson at the very beginning of my POW experience, and I did not fully realize this until I read Frankl's book. What he said resonated with me and helped me to understand how, perhaps innately, I had responded to my circumstances as a prisoner. This is what continues to guide me, to this very day, every day. I often need help from others, especially from Marty, my best friend, companion, and guide, but in the end, each choice is mine.

I learned a second great lesson from my experience, but it did not come until the very end. As I wrote in my journal, when I walked through the gates of the Hanoi Hilton on February 12, 1973, as we were leaving the prison that had symbolized all the misery and hatred that we had endured over those many years, I turned to face the compound and said, "I forgive you." I did that because I knew I could not and should not carry that hatred back home with me, back to my family and my life of freedom. I realized during the last few hours of my captivity that although hatred had been useful as part of the armor that had protected me from the influence of my captors, it was no longer needed. Hatred is a poison to the soul, mind, and body, and it has been the source of many of the ills in the world throughout most of our history.

When I walked through those gates and said those words, I was freed from *two* prisons. It was the most liberating act of my life, and I chose to do it. One must *choose* to forgive.

Boots in Hanoi

It was March 2005, and Marty and I were back in Hanoi, leading a university alumni group on a tour of Vietnam. Since the last time I had been there, in 1998, the traffic had increased dramatically, and there were many other changes.

Just as I was about to hop into the shower, the phone in my Metropole Hotel room rang. This was after a full day of roaming around Hanoi, learning how to cross the streets filled with motorbikes and cars and no stoplights, searching the shops for a certain type of chopstick box that my friend Jaybee Souder wanted, and once again trying to get the feel of the city that had been such a part of my life.

"Hello," I said, expecting it to be one of my friends in the group. "Hi, this is Bill Bainbridge," the caller said, "and Doug Reese gave me your name and said that I could reach you here. I am a reporter for the *Deutsche Presse-Agentur*, and I am writing a story on the thirtieth anniversary of the end of the war that is coming up, and I was hoping to be able to interview you." After some discussion, I agreed to meet him.

"Tomorrow the tour group will be going to the Army Museum, and I could give you some time if you can meet us there at ten," I told him. "And one other thing," I added, "I will be looking to find my flight boots in the museum."

I had seen my boots there on my first trip back to Vietnam, in 1998, after my friend Irv Williams spotted them with my name written on the inside. That was some thirty-three years after I had last seen them being pulled from my feet by the crowd of villagers who had captured me north of Hanoi in October 1965. I was anxious to see if they were still on display and, if so, to ask for their return. The twenty-two people in the group that we were leading had all heard this story and were curious as well. Most of the group were alumni from Queens and Davidson and their friends. Queens University was Marty's alma mater and Davidson College was mine, and we were the official "tour guides" along with our Vietnamese guide and interpreter. My childhood friend Bill Thompson, now a Queens faculty member, had done a lot of organizing for the trip. Marty was the real guide, since she had planned the itinerary, having spent considerable time in Vietnam on three different occasions. She had been back in 2002 and 2004 without me. On the last trip, she volunteered at Hoa Sua School, teaching English to disadvantaged youth. Dabney joined her there for Tet, the lunar new year. On both trips, Marty had looked for the boots in the museum and had not found them.

This time, in March 2005, Quan, our affable Vietnamese guide, was anxious to show off the MiG-21 on display outside the museum, since he was a former MiG-21 pilot, but too young to have fought in the war, which was known as the Vietnam War to us and as the American War to them.

Bill was waiting by the MiG when we arrived the next morning and, after posing for a photo with Quan and the MiG, I did the short interview.

The museum was quite different from what I remembered, and no one had yet reported finding the boots. I had about given up when I just happened to notice a darkened, clear plastic display case beside the Russian T-34 tank that dominated the room. Sure enough, way in the back of the case were my boots, looking as though someone had put a coat of polish on them.

"Hey guys, here they are!" I shouted. The group quickly came running. However, it was dark there and difficult for photography, so I asked Quan to find someone in the museum who could give me permission to take them out of the case so we could take pictures.

Shortly, Quan came back with two guys dressed in Vietnamese army uniforms, one of them a colonel who was introduced as the assistant director. Then began a rather serious and formal questioning about who I was and how I knew these boots were mine. I was thinking, *This is another damn interrogation, and I am not at all sure I want to go through with this*, but I swallowed the bile in my throat and provided the information truthfully, putting down "teacher" as my profession. Do I tell them I teach at the Naval War College? Maybe not a good idea at this point, so I write "Queens," that being what was on the sign on the bus we arrived in.

Now satisfied that I was the "Halyburton" of boots fame, the Vietnamese accorded me dignitary status and asked me to sit in one of the two "official meeting" chairs, which were arranged just like the ones you have probably seen of Chairman Mao and Prime Minister So-and-So, with the coffee table between them, and the little tea service set on top. After more questions and more stiff politeness, I asked if I could take the boots out.

"The director must give permission for that, and he is attending a conference," Quan explained. "However, we have sent for him, and he is on his way." He added that the director was a very famous war hero who fought in the South for many years. That probably meant that he had killed a lot of Americans, but I chose to look beyond this reality and think about the present.

The director finally arrived. There were introductions, questions, polite pleasantries. Wow, this was turning into a big production. "May we see the boots now?" I asked. "We are waiting for the official photographer," Quan answered. Finally, the photographer arrived and someone opened the case and the boots were in my hands. There was my name—on the inside top of each boot—and I could see all the letters for the first time. They felt a little gritty, even though they seemed to have been cleaned and polished since I last saw them. I remember thinking at the time that they looked like some Vietnamese peasant had been wearing

During a visit to the Vietnamese Army Museum after the war, Porter holds the flight boots that his captors took when he ejected from his crippled aircraft. Bearing his name inside, they had been on display for years. He never was able to persuade Vietnamese authorities to return them.

them in the rice paddies for quite a while before turning them over to authorities.

I posed with the boots, with the director, with the assistant director, with Marty, and with Quan, who seemed to be enjoying all this attention. In front of us, it looked like a mob of paparazzi. By now the event had drawn an additional crowd from the other museum visitors and staff. The director seemed quite pleased with all the attention, and things got more relaxed and friendly. *Now is the time to ask for the boots*, I thought.

"Oh no, that would not be possible, since these objects are on loan and cannot be given away," the director said.

"Okay, how about my Rolex?" I asked.

This brought a laugh, but in the next breath the director said that he had "many other things of yours in another place" and that I could see them when I come back.

"John McCain visited the museum and was given all of his things," I countered. I knew this was true since I had seen them on display in the National Aviation Museum in Pensacola. Quite diplomatically I did not point out the contradiction contained in these statements.

As we prepared to leave and the boots were back in their place, the director asked for a special photo of the two of us in front of the tank and then another of our entire group. We exchanged business cards. Colonel Le Ma Luong must have been rewarded with this cushy position for his long and heroic service in the South.

For the final scene of this little drama, I was asked to sign the guest book and make a comment about our visit. More reluctant diplomacy, paving the way for a future visit.

In the spring of 2009, leading another travel group to Vietnam, I had prepared the way with a letter to the Army Museum director, telling him we were coming and would like to visit and see the boots. When we arrived, we were greeted with considerable pomp and ceremony. The director and several other army officers were in their dress uniforms, the women in our group each received a bouquet of roses, and we were escorted into a formal conference room.

At the head of a handsome long conference table, resplendent with flower arrangements and set for tea, was a platform with my flight boots. Hanging at the end of the room was a portrait of Ho Chi Minh.

I was more hopeful on this visit, our third. We had now had the obligatory three cups of tea with dignitaries, so I was convinced that must have softened their position about the boots. It became clear that I was wrong when it was explained through an interpreter that I must submit four letters requesting the return of the boots—to the museum director, to the heads of their army, to their foreign ministry, and to another office I do not remember. They also requested something in return, specifically American antiwar memorabilia. That was a price I was unwilling to pay.

At this, I stood up and told the group that we were leaving, which we did, much to the consternation of the Vietnamese officials. As we were looking at other items in the museum, our interpreter came running to say that the director wanted me to return to the room. I thought surely he had changed his mind and would give me the boots. Instead, there was a Japanese film crew there, and I was told they were making a documentary about Vietnamese aces (pilots who have shot down five or more enemy aircraft) from the "American War."

One of these "aces" was in the room with us. He was a little guy wearing an ill-fitting sport coat and a gaudy tie, but was quite friendly as we were introduced. Again, we conversed through our interpreter, and he proceeded to describe, along with the appropriate

Visiting the Vietnamese Army Museum in 2009, Porter swaps fighter stories with former enemy pilot Luu Huy Chao, who claimed to have shot five American jets out of the skies in his MiG-17F fighter. As it turned out, he got only one aircraft—a slow-moving RC-47 cargo plane. Tiep Thi *magazine, September 2009*

aviator hand motions, just how he had shot down these five American jet fighters. After he had finished, I told him, "You know, back in 1965, you MiG pilots would never come up to fight, even though we gave you plenty of opportunities, and we could never figure out why. If you had come up to fight, I would have probably shot you down." I'm not sure how that was translated to him, but we both had a big laugh and shook hands.

Several days later I searched "Vietnamese Aces" on the internet and found a spreadsheet that listed all sixteen of them, along with the number of aircraft claimed and the number verified. There was my pilot, next to the bottom, with six claimed, but only one—an

RC-47 reconnaissance plane—confirmed. So, the truth was that Luu Huy Chao had jumped this large, slow-moving cargo plane, probably over Laos, in his MiG-17F. I'm sure it was a hell of a dogfight! I am just sorry I did not know this when I was introduced to him.

Overall, the Vietnamese inflated the number of kills by 60 percent, and there were only three confirmed aces. I have given up trying to get my boots back.

Hoa Lo Prison Museum

Today, Hoa Lo, Maison Centrale, the Hanoi Hilton, whatever name you wish to call it, is a museum occupying only a small portion of the original prison complex. The prison had occupied an entire city block, and most of it was torn down to make room for Hanoi's first modern high-rise building. In the high-rise there are apartments, offices, shops, and restaurants. Initially the museum focused on Vietnamese "patriots" imprisoned there by the French, but the small section about American POWs was of interest to many tourists, and so over the years, that has been substantially expanded.

Marty and I have been back to Vietnam quite a few times since that initial trip in 1998, and on one of them, before visiting the Hoa Lo Prison Museum again, we had breakfast in a very swanky restaurant on the seventh floor of that high-rise. With some visual calculations, I was able to determine that we were eating this delicious breakfast over the spot where Cell No. 2 of Camp Unity had been, and where I had spent so much time eating much poorer fare.

The museum stretches off to the left of the high rise and this part of Hoa Lo contains the main entrance, with the remnants of Little Vegas and New Guy Village on either side. The dried up moat is on the street behind the wall, and now it is filled with displays and a gift shop.

As I complete this tapestry of stories about my years in prison, we are approaching fifty years since the end of the war and my release. I have been writing these remembrances off and on for more than thirty of them. As they now come together, I am struck by the realization that, taken together, my time and experiences as a POW have shaped and guided my life in a very positive way. I hope that I have been able to convey some of the how and the why of this, but the most powerful thing I am left with is a deep sense of gratitude and a desire to pass these lessons along to others. I have tried to do this through the hundreds of lectures, speeches, and presentations that I have given over the years, and I hope this collection of stories will do that as well.

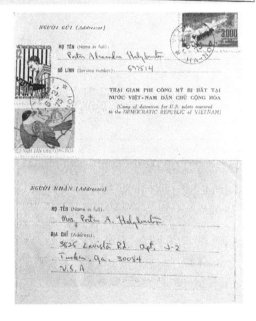

(*Top*) Porter's last letter to Marty before release, written on the seven-line letter form POWs had to use.

(*Bottom*) The reverse side of the letter above. Note the two stamps commemorating the downing of the 3,000th and the 3,500th American aircraft—known as "May Bay My." These numbers greatly exceed the actual number of aircraft lost in North Vietnam.

APPENDIX

List of American POWs Mentioned in This Book

The sixty-three American POWs mentioned in this book (in order of appearance).

As listed in this book	*Full name and rank as POW*
Stan Olmstead	Lt. Cdr. Stanley E. Olmstead, USN
Tubby Johnson	Lt. Robert W. Johnson, USN
Zipper Ward	Lt. (jg) Wayne Ward, USN
Fred Cherry	Maj. Fred V. Cherry, USAF
Dave Wheat	Lt. (jg) David R. Wheat, USN
Jim Stockdale	Cdr. James B. Stockdale, USN
Duffy Hutton	Lt. (jg) James L. Hutton, USN
Jim Bell	Lt. James F. "Jim" Bell, USN
Ralph Gaither	Ens. Ralph E. Gaither, USN
Rod Knutson	Lt. (jg) Rodney A. Knutson, USN
Porter Halyburton	Lt. (jg) Porter A. Halyburton, USN
Jerry Denton	Cdr. Jeremiah A. Denton, USN
Art Burer	Capt. Arthur W. Burer, USAF
Red Berg	1st Lt. Kile D. Berg, USAF
Howie Dunn	Maj. John H. Dunn, USMC
Warrant Officer "Freddie" Frederick	CWO2 John W. Frederick, USMC
John Dramesi	Capt. John A. Dramesi, USAF
Ed Atterberry	Capt. Edwin Atterberry, USAF
Harley Chapman	Capt. Harlan P. Chapman, USMC
Everett Alvarez	Lt. (jg) Everett Alvarez Jr., USN

Bill Tschudy	Lt. (jg) William M. Tschudy, USN
Robbie Risner	Lt. Col. Robinson Risner, USAF
Paul Kari	Capt. Paul A. Kari, USAF
J. B. McKamey	Lt. John B. McKamey, USN
Dick Ratzlaff	Lt. (jg) Richard R. Ratzlaff, USN
Al Carpenter	Lt. Allen R. Carpenter, USN
Bob Purcell	Capt. Robert B. Purcell, USAF
Glenn Daigle	Lt. (jg) Glenn H. Daigle, USN
Irv Williams	Lt. (jg) Lewis I. Williams, USN
Mike Christian	Lt. (jg) Michael D. Christian, USN
Fred Purrington	Lt. (jg) Frederick R. Purrington, USN
Tom Browning	1st Lt. Ralph T. Browning, USAF
Don Spoon	1st Lt. Donald R. Spoon, USAF
Gary Sigler	1st Lt. Gary R. Sigler, USAF
Jack Davies	1st Lt. John O. Davies, USAF
Red McDaniel	Lt. Cdr. Eugene B. McDaniel, USN
Ed Davis	Lt. (jg) Edward A. Davis, USN
Bunny Talley	1st Lt. Bernard L. Talley, USAF
Marty Neuens	1st Lt. Martin J. Neuens, USAF
Bill Shankel	Lt. (jg) William L. Shankel, USN
Jerry Singleton	1st Lt. Jerry A. Singleton, USAF
Bert Campbell	1st Lt. Burton W. Campbell, USAF
Al Lurie	Capt. Alan P. Lurie, USAF
Mike McGrath	Lt. John M. McGrath, USN
Phil Butler	Lt. Phillip N. Butler, USN
Hubie Buchanan	1st Lt. Hubert E. Buchanan, USAF
John Savast	Maj. John E. Stavast, USAF
Smitty Harris	Capt. Carlyle S. Harris, USAF
Quincy Collins	1st Lt. James Q. Collins, USAF
John Flynn	Col. John Flynn, USAF
John Borling	1st Lt. John L. Borling, USAF
Glen Nix	Capt. Cowan G. Nix, USAF
Larry Guarino	Maj. Lawrence N. Guarino, USAF

Kay Russell	Lt. Cdr. Kay Russell, USN
Bob Shumaker	Lt. Cdr. Robert H. Shumaker, USN
Dave Hatcher	Capt. David B. Hatcher, USAF
Brian Woods	Lt. Cdr. Brian W. Woods, USN
Wilber	Cdr. Walter E. Wilber, USN
Miller	Lt. Col. Edison W. Miller, USMC
Ray Vohden	Lt. Cdr. Raymond A. Vohden, USN
Jim Parrie	Lt. Cdr. James Parrie, USN
Wendell Alcorn	Lt. (jg) Wendell R. Alcorn, USN
Brad Smith	Lt. Bradley E. Smith, USN

NOTES

Introduction

1. The Vietnam War was all about communism and part of the Cold War strategy to stop its spread by Red (Mainland) China and the Soviet Union. After World War II, the French had tried to reassert their control over their former colonies in Indochina, but they were opposed by Ho Chi Minh, who had declared Vietnam's independence in 1945 following the defeat of Japan. The United States inherited the war from France in 1954, after that country's defeat at Dien Bien Phu by Ho Chi Minh's communist Viet Minh forces. The peace treaty temporarily divided the country into two parts, north and south, at the seventeenth parallel, with eventual reunification to be decided by popular vote in 1956. This vote did not take place because the United States feared that Ho would win, and Washington opposed any further spread of communism following China's fall to Mao Tse-tung in 1949. America's involvement was gradual, and evolved into three wars—the anti-guerrilla fight against the Viet Cong insurgents in the South; the more conventional war against the regular North Vietnamese Army in the South; and the air war against the North, designed to stop the flow of troops and supplies into the South via the Ho Chi Minh Trail through Laos and Cambodia. The overall mission of the Navy's carrier force in 1965 was to prevent those supplies from reaching the Trail.

2. The F-4B was the Navy version of McDonnell Mach 2 Phantom II fighter, designed in 1958 as a "do-all" aircraft. During its thirty-one-year service life, the Phantom also was used by the U.S. Air Force and Marine Corps and the air arms of several foreign countries. The squadron designation of VF-84 indicated that ours was a fixed-wing fighter squadron, which usually comprised twelve aircraft.

Part One. Rolling with the Punches

1. The U.S. Armed Forces Code of Conduct was established in August 1955, following the experience of POWs in the Korean War. It was intended to provide a concise guide for the conduct and responsibilities of U.S. service members should they be faced with capture or imprisonment during war. The following is the original version and the one that SERE School used in my training and in that of others of that era. It was hammered into me that I should be willing to die rather than give more than is permitted in Article V. It was the training that was in error because the article was intended to *require* you to provide this information to your captors so that you prove that you, as a POW, come under the protection of the Geneva Conventions of 1949. This misinterpretation in our training in the Code caused many of us a great deal of pain and suffering. After Vietnam, the word "bound" was replaced with "required," and the word "only" was removed from Article V to clarify this point. In 1988, gender-specific language was removed from the Code.

The Code of Conduct (version in force in 1965 and 1967)

I.   I am an American fighting man. I serve in the forces which guard my country and our way of life. I am prepared to give my life in their defense.

II.   I will never surrender of my own free will. If in command, I will never surrender my men while they still have the means to resist.

III. If I am captured I will continue to resist by all means available. I will make every effort to escape and aid others to escape. I will accept neither parole nor special favors from the enemy.

IV.   If I become a prisoner of war, I will keep faith with my fellow prisoners. I will give no information or take part in any action which might be harmful to my comrades. If I am senior, I will take command. If not, I will obey the lawful orders of those appointed over me and will back them up in every way.

V.   When questioned, should I become a prisoner of war, I am bound to give only name, rank, service number and date of birth. I will evade answering further questions to the utmost of my ability. I will make no oral or written statements disloyal to my country and its allies or harmful to their cause.

VI. I will never forget that I am an American fighting man, responsible for my actions, and dedicated to the principles which made my country free. I will trust in my God and in the United States of America.

2. For more information, see the section "Killed in Action" later in this chapter.

3. Edgar Allen Poe, "The Cask of Amontillado," *New England Weekly Review*, Nov. 1846.

4. The Gong was a kind of bell made from a variety of metal objects that resonated when struck, like an artillery shell. It was used to signal reveille and taps in the way a bugle is and there was a very distinctive pattern to it. The Gong was also used as an alarm device.

5. For more about this, see the section "Fred Cherry's Ordeal" later in this chapter.

6. For a much more complete account of my time with Fred Cherry see James S. Hirsch, *Two Souls Indivisible: The Friendship That Saved Two POWs in Vietnam* (New York: Houghton Mifflin, 2004).

7. For a definitive account of the March see Gary Wayne Foster, *The Hanoi March: American POWs in North Vietnam's Crucible* (Ashland, OR: Hellgate Press, 2022).

8. For the Stockdale story, see Jim and Sybil Stockdale, *In Love and War: The Story of a Family's Ordeal and Sacrifice During the Vietnam Years* (New York: Harper & Row, 1984).

9. Stockdale, 191–208.

Part Two. Surviving

1. Sgt. Edgar Halyburton was from Iredell County, North Carolina, and was with the first group of U.S. soldiers sent to France in World War I under the command of U.S. Army general John Pershing. While training in trench warfare, Sergeant Halyburton and eleven others were captured by the Germans as the first U.S. POWs. He spent a year in various prisons and became a strong leader and organizer in each of them. General Pershing, presented him with the Distinguished Service Medal—the first ever conferred on an enlisted man. He was in the 16th Infantry, Company F.

His citation from the War Department read

> Sgt. Edgar Halyburton, while a prisoner in the hands of the German government from Nov 3rd 1917 to Nov 1918, voluntarily took command of the different camps in which he was located and under difficult conditions, established administrative and personal headquarters, organized the men into units, billeted them systematically, established sanitary regulations, made equitable distribution of supplies and established an intelligence service to prevent our men from giving information to the enemy and prevented the enemy from introducing propaganda.

After the war he wrote a book called *Shoot and Be Damned*. His photograph was also used on a Liberty Loan poster to support the military. https://www.findagrave.com/memorial/3714166/edgar-morrison-halyburton (August 14, 2021).

2. For the full account of the escape, see George Hayward, *The Party Dolls: The True, Tragic Story of Two Americans' Attempted Escape from a Hanoi POW Camp* (independently published, 2021).

ABOUT THE AUTHOR

Porter Alexander Halyburton spent twenty years on active duty in the U.S. Navy, retiring as a commander in 1984. He spent another twenty years on the faculty of the Naval War College, retiring as Professor of Strategy Emeritus in 2006. Among his many medals and awards, he received the Silver Star for "conspicuous gallantry and intrepidity" while interned. Porter is a potter, woodworker, poet, public speaker, and traveler. He still possesses the tombstone that his mother had placed in the family plot when he was declared KIA and says that he likes looking down on it rather than up from it. He and Marty, his wife of nearly sixty years, have three grown children and one grandson.

CPSIA information can be obtained
at www.ICGtesting.com
Printed in the USA
LVHW080940300123
738206LV00018B/165/J

9 781682 478257